Accessible Judaism:
A Concise Guide

www.guidetojudaism.com

Rabbi Jacques Cukierkorn

Accessible Judaism:
A Concise Guide

www.guidetojudaism.com

Printed by
BooksJustBooks.com

In cooperation with
Solving Light Books

Cover design
Álvaro Gómez

Layout
Álvaro Gómez

International Standard Book Number (ISBN)
Paper:
Printed in the United States of America

Dedication

To my daughters Raquel and Dahlia, and to my wife Denisse. If it wasn't for the fact that she is Jewish, should have been canonized already!

This book would not have been possible without the support and motivation I received from my many students and friends. I would particularly like to thank my collaborator Michael Boekstal, my editor Michael Peluse, Paul Uhlmann Jr., Lawrence Starr, Michael Rosenblum, and Andrew Starr and Father George Balasko for their help, encouragement, and many hours dedicated to this book.

I would also like to express my gratitude to Mr. Robert Uhlmann and family, not only for their generous financial support for the editing of this book, but primarily for sharing my ideals.

Contents

Introduction

I was born in Brazil to what in Sao Paulo is considered "a good Ashkenazi Jewish family." Since I belonged to such a family, it went without saying that I attended Jewish Day school and joined Jewish youth groups like B'nei Akiva and Netzach. I was somewhere around sixteen when a boy from Northern Brazil showed up at one of those youth groups. Joao was his name. Joao claimed to be a descendant of secret Jews and he wanted to "return home," he wanted to be recognized as a member of the fold. For this Joao had come to Sao Paulo, a large Jewish community. And he had created everything he thought he needed to lead a Jewish life, including a self-made kippa and tallit.

Don't think that Joao found any welcome. Neither for him, nor for the thousands of other crypto-Jews in northern Brazil was it very easy to be recognized. Even though, or maybe because, they had founded their own synagogues and other institutions.

From early childhood on I had heard stories about descendants of Portuguese and Spanish Jews who could only save their lives by converting to Christianity, yet remained practicing Jews in secret. The idea of invisible crypto-Jews wanting to return to official Judaism and become full-fledged Jews, has inspired writers of all times. But it was never thought of something that would actually happen. And there was Joao with his unbreakable will to be Jewish, for he felt that he couldn't be anything else.

Joao told us remarkable stories of crypto-Jewish communities in remote and poor Northern Brazil. Years later I wrote my rabbinical thesis on these crypto-Jews and I greatly enjoyed the honor of officiating at their synagogues. Even today I am still tied to them thanks to Kulanu, the worldwide organization that concerns itself with lost and dispersed Jewish communities.

With his stories about his community and his desire, Joao was the symbol of a painful paradox. Throughout history millions of people have been tortured, humiliated and sacrificed under the accusation of being Jews. Yet when the survivors of history and their descendants have knocked on the doors of those they considered to be their brothers, those doors were and often still are slammed shut. How is this possible? In the name of what? Since the early beginning the wise men of Jewish tradition have developed laws and formulas for returning to Judaism without being held accountable for the sins of our ancestors. So how can we not have an open door towards sincere people who find themselves in a situation they did not choose?

Too much time has gone by, some will say. But apparently not for those who seek to return. 500 years ago their Judaism wasn't accepted by their neighbors. Now their Judaism isn't accepted by their own family. Joao made me relive some of the chapters of Jewish history. His was the voice of the Jews of Morocco who had to convert to Islam to save their lives in the 13th century, terribly affected by their apostasy, writing letters to Maimonides in search of encouragement, feeling guilty for not having chosen martyrdom. In Joao's words echo the voices of the Jews in England, who were expelled for more than three centuries, after years of blood libel charges, having to wear a yellow badge and a gradual restriction of their rights.

Isn't there constant change and renovation in Judaism to let the Jewish people survive? Shouldn't we be gentle and humane to the children of those who have suffered as Jews? Ever since then I have wanted to speak with a gentle and humane voice on behalf of Joao, in favor of change and renovation.

Don't get me wrong, I am not interested in proselytizing. Judaism does not seek to convert anyone; neither do I. It is not due to arrogance. I am deeply convinced that it is the task of us all, Jews and non-Jews alike, to make this world more humane. I have reached that conclusion through Judaism, that's my identity and I struggle every day to maintain it. At the same time I am fully aware that there are many compasses that help us search for a more humane world. And they don't have to be all religious, nor do they need to be predetermined by birth.

In my work as a rabbi I often meet people in a situation similar to Joao's. Non-Jewish people who happen to fall in love with a Jew, who want their children to be raised Jewish in spite of their different background. They find closed doors, as if sincerely loving somebody is somehow an unforgivable transgression. Just like I meet children with only a Jewish father who are rejected by the Jewish community, and gays and lesbians whose choice of partner becomes a pejorative measure of their human virtues and their commitment to the community... All of these men and women are human first.

From the very beginning I have viewed my task as a rabbi as building bridges for those who sincerely want to make Judaism the prism through which to see the world, the way of life they want to lead, freely and independently. With this desire to build bridges of understanding I have written this guide to values and practices of modern Judaism: so that you will have a basic roadmap when you want to explore Judaism, whether it is something long forgotten or new territory for you.

A guide like this shouldn't be necessary. In a world where two out of three synagogues are non-Orthodox, there should be more than enough options, for the Jew wishing to return to his or her origins and the proselyte alike. But unfortunately the opposite is true. Judaism is depleting itself by not providing the answers the majority of Jews are looking for and assimilation continues increasing at a breathtaking pace. And at the same many Jews who remain faithful hold on to a defensive idea of Judaism that in its most excessive form is portrayed by the excluding, radical Ultra-Orthodox groups who look with suspicion on anything they can't call their own. Their view is defying the Jewish tradition of dialogue, search for consensus, variety and debate, the very hallmarks that has helped Judaism survive against the odds. Now that this guide is here, I will feel rewarded if only one of you finds his or her way independently to the Jewish fold.

During the Passover Seder, Jews open the doors of their homes. We relate this custom to the prophet Eliyahu, although there are theories that it is rooted in the times when Christians accused the Jews of murdering Christian children to make matzah. By opening their doors, the Jews showed their world. Everybody could pass by. Anyone could step in. I hope that this book is such an open door. I'd like to show you what we Jews believe in. These are our traditions, this is our history. This is who we are. This is where we differ among ourselves. We will be very honored to receive you as equals and to recognize the ties that bind us.

Do you wonder whatever happened to Joao? Shortly after my ordination I took a short trip to Israel an, as I was walking up to the Western Wall, somebody screamed my name. A man dressed in black, with sidelocks, a beard and a hat approached me. It took me a while to recognize him under all the hair and clothes. It was Joao.

Joao was very upset with me. It was very hot and I was dressed accordingly: in shorts and a T-shirt. He didn't understand how I could be so irreverent in such a holy place; I either had to cover myself or leave. And I felt happy. Somehow I had helped him find his own Jewish identity, although it had little or nothing to do with my own.

There are many, many ways to live your Judaism. Find yours.

Kansas City, December 15, 2003

Editor's Note

Why publish another book on Judaism? There is already an abundance of titles available on virtually any Jewish-related topic. But it is also true that there are still many gaps. Primarily, the majority of extant books deal with Judaism from a particular angle; that is, they preach a very specific vision of Judaism, a vision at times more concerned about itself than with the subject at hand. It is still sadly hard to find a book which, in one volume, deals with a wide scope of topics. There is a high demand for a book which gives a general idea of Judaism, seen from different angles. *Accessible Judaism* hopes to fill this gap.

Although the author is well known as a Reform rabbi, he grew up in the Orthodox tradition, and is thus familiar with the Jewish world from opposite angles. *Accessible Judaism* makes the first serious attempt to approach Judaism in an inclusive way, offering as many points of view on a given topic as possible. We believe that this inclusive approach is more interesting and educational for the reader. It's an invitation for him or her to understand Judaism and arrive at his or her own conclusions-

We also feel that it is important to offer in one accessible volume a comprehensive "manual" of Judaism, a book that explores a wide array of topics, divided into self-containing, easily readable chapters. In that way, the reader can start at the beginning or choose a specific topic at any point.

The manual idea is reinforced by the At-a-Glance sections at the end of each thematic section. It offers useful information related to each topic. The reader can consult it either before reading the section, in order to get a clearer idea about the type of information covered, or after reading the section, as a conclusion or synthesis.

At the back of the book there is an extensive appendix section, which extends the topics covered earlier, such as the differences between Christianity and Judaism, prayers, and so on.

In short, *Accessible Judaism* was written for readers, Jewish and Gentile, who are approaching Judaism and are searching for a book that answers all their questions. It hopes to offer a comprehensive outlook through both the variety of topics covered and the breadth of its treatment of those topics. In doing so, it demands that the reader take an active role and think critically about Judaism, so that he or she may choose his or her own path. More than a "Chosen People," Judaism will be enriched if it truly becomes a "Choosing People."

Jewish History

Introduction

"All things are mortal but the Jew; all other forces pass, but he remains. What is the secret of his immortality?" (Mark Twain)

When we look at the history of the Jews, it seems full of contradictions. Counting for less than one percent of the world's population at any given time, their contribution to the world is nearly immeasurable. Although Jews have always been a dissenting minority, rejecting polytheism, idolatry and the subsequent religions that surrounded them, Western ethical thinking is based on the earliest Jewish scriptures. Inspired by the Ten Commandments and the Torah as a whole, the notion of how we ought to act towards those who are less fortunate than us, our sense of social responsibility and the moral imperative of sharing the wealth we have even though it might only be relative wealth compared to the fortune of others, is originally Jewish. Judaism is the parent of the two major religions in the world: Christianity and Islam.

Jewish history can't be discussed without reference to racism, bigotry, expulsion, torture, murder, pogroms, and genocide. However, while these words carve out the saddest of memories, another enigma emerges. Is there any other minority that has suffered so many threats to its existence and yet has managed to survive? As a matter of fact, there are only two other cultures that are of comparable antiquity to the Jews: the Chinese, who have survived because of their large numbers and geographical isolation, and the Hindus, who have survived because of their large numbers and syncretism.

Most of the cultures that brutally diminished the Jewish population have long ceased to exist, like the Babylonians and Assyrians. All of the empires that tried to change the Jew into something he was not have vanished: Rome is just a city, Greece and Spain are just countries. The Jews have even survived the greatest crime history has ever witnessed: six million Jews found their end in the gas chambers of Auschwitz, Treblinka, and Sobibor. But the Jews are still around. Not downtrodden and hidden, but dignified and proud. With the State of Israel as the ultimate symbol of its enduring survival and as the ultimate response to the monstrosities of the Holocaust.

Although Jews have always been a dissenting minority, rejecting polytheism, idolatry and the subsequent religions that surrounded them, Western ethical thinking is based on the earliest Jewish scriptures.

With the revival of Hebrew as a vernacular language after 2,000 years of exclusively religious use, as a hallmark of a vibrant history defying culture.

In trying to disclose the secret of Jewish "immortality," there is probably no single, definite answer. Some might say God's protection of God's chosen people must play a part in it. That is a troubling notion. For if God is willing and able to interfere so directly in the survival of a people, the question of why God would allow for so much suffering arises. A God who lets a people survive just to make it suffer is not a God we want to envision. Historic coincidence can't be an answer either, for it would be too much coincidence, it defies all logic and statistics.

In search for an explanation, another paradox appears. Maybe the Jews have managed to survive as a people bound by a common culture because for most of their history they lacked everything that defines a nation and a culture.

First of all, after the destruction of the second Temple the Jews were left without a geographical center. For centuries, the date of the destruction (*Tisha b'Av*) was commemorated as a day of mourning and today that is still how Orthodox Jews experience this event. One could wonder whether this is the appropriate way to approach this date, since a case could be made that the destruction of the physical center of Jewish spiritual life might very well be what has saved the Jewish people. Every nation, every culture, every religion that has expressed its existence through material means has vanished while the Jews were forced to reinvent their religion into a religion of ideas, of concepts. Lightweight, portable and applicable everywhere in the world, allowing the Jews to settle on all of the five continents while they could bring their identity with them. From the valleys of Yemen to the shtetls in Poland, from the banks of the Ganges and the Amazon to the Lower East Side in Manhattan.

In the second place, the Jews have never been bothered by a central authority in post-Talmudic times. While the weakening of a central authority is usually the first sign of the demise of a nation, the Jews were never confronted with this inevitability of history. If there was any hierarchy of power, it never exceeded the local or regional level, thus ensuring that if one region declined in importance, the Jewish people as a whole were not

Every nation, every culture, every religion that has expressed its existence through material means has vanished while the Jews were forced to reinvent their religion into a religion of ideas, of concepts.

Jews have never been bothered by a central authority in post-Talmudic times.

threatened in their existence. If one wants to make a case for democracy, that person should point out how Jews have always built their communities. It can even be taken a step further. Those with influence were traditionally rabbis, given merit and respect for their erudition. One could even say that the structure of Jewish communities has always reflected Plato's ideals of the perfect society.

These two hallmarks of Jewish identity throughout most of history, the absence of a geographical, material focus and of central authority, gave the Jews the flexibility to survive, to be part of nine major civilizations and societies. Jewish religion is virtually without any dogma, but for the paradigm that there is only one God. However, nowhere in what the Jews consider to be the Bible does it state one has to believe in that God. Thus, Jewish thought is open to interpretation in an unparalleled way. Everyone is free to find a view within Judaism that is meaningful to him or her, and the fluidity of Judaism within the vessel of monotheism has saved it from the "make or break" mechanism that has been the downfall of many ideologies and religions.

No Jew can tell another Jew how or what to believe, something that becomes most evident in the richest source of Jewish knowledge, the Talmud. When exploring the Talmud, one will not find unequivocal quotes or rulings on legal and moral matters, but rather a collection of debates and discussions by various rabbis on different subjects. What the Talmud tells us is that from its earliest days on, Judaism has always permitted various opinions to exist next to each other.

This continuous process of individual interpretation has allowed Judaism to renew itself from within whenever the times demanded it. When new scientific discoveries or philosophical theories proved themselves too important to ignore, Judaism knew how to adapt. When changing geopolitical circumstances forced Jews into the ghetto or brought them into general society, Judaism knew how to respond. But Judaism did not only know how to react to external factors; it also responded to needs from within.

We find adaptation to local needs in the difference in prayer books, for instance. In Ashkenazi, Eastern European prayer books we find fewer prayers for rain and dew than in Sefardi prayer books from Mediterranean

Jewish religion is virtually without any dogma, but for the paradigm that there is only one God.

No Jew can tell another Jew how or what to believe, something that becomes most evident in the richest source of Jewish knowledge, the Talmud.

countries, where precipitation is much more of a life and death matter than in other climates. Still today, a prayer for the royal family in the Portuguese language can be found in the prayer book of the long-standing Sefardi community in the Netherlands, reflecting the historic fact that the Lowlands were the only place where Jews were welcome after their expulsion from the Iberian peninsula.

Throughout the ages, Judaism has always embraced change and has thus safeguarded its core, even when changes were forced by spiritual, philosophical or theological revolutions.

Throughout the ages, Judaism has always embraced change and has thus safeguarded its core, even when changes were forced by spiritual, philosophical or theological revolutions. Hassidism, for instance, was a radical break with the intellectual approach to Judaism and sought a more direct emotional experience. It is not too far-fetched to state that the Hassidic movement was the Reform Judaism of its founding days. Although other shifts in Judaism might not have been as dramatic, the fact remains that Judaism has never been frozen in time, allowing it to survive until the moment Jews became citizens of the countries they lived in or at least could benefit from civil rights.

In the Beginning:
From Early Dawn to 200 C.E.

The First Jewish Commonwealth: 1200-588 B.C.E.

Although many critical-historical Bible scholars have different theories on the dawn of Judaism and a case can be made that the Exodus out of Egypt never took place or that it is questionable whether Moses ever existed, this is not a critical-historical book. The following account of Jewish history is not meant to be scientific, but it is how we as Jews perceive and trace our origins from our central collection of texts, the Torah.

The Jewish people began as a small family tribe under the leadership of Abraham. They were called the Hebrew tribe and were kept together by a firm belief in one God. "Hebrew" literally means "from the other side," as Abraham and his family came from a different place. Abraham's leadership was passed on to Isaac, who in turn was succeeded by Jacob. Toward the death of Jacob, the Hebrews settled in Egypt. There they were cruelly enslaved by the Pharaohs for a long period until they were redeemed from slavery by the great leader and prophet, Moses.

"Hebrew" literally means "from the other side," as Abraham and his family came from a different place.

Freedom was only the first step. The Israelites (literally "children of Israel," i.e. "descendants of Jacob") who marched out of Egypt were still slaves in mind. The turbulent and revolutionary murmuring against Moses in the desert proved that they were not quite ready to become the people of God, and it took forty years in the wilderness before a new generation of strong men and women were ready for national independence. It was the giving of the Torah which marked the greatest moment in their shaping as a people. It presented them with a national and ideal way of life. It prepared them to embark upon the third stage of their development: entering into a land they could call their own.

It was the giving of the Torah which marked the greatest moment in their shaping as a people.

The Israelites conquered territory east of the Jordan before Moses died. His successor, the soldier Joshua, led his people over the Jordan. After taking Jericho, they invaded the hill country and struggled bitterly with the local tribes before gaining mastery of the land. In that very beginning of settlement, the Israelites did not possess a solid block of land within Canaan, but were scattered over the region.

The various peoples that inhabited Canaan were never decisively defeated and continued to live with and around the Israelites. This presented two great dangers to them: danger of attack and the danger of assimilation. The great enemies of the time were mainly the Canaanites, Midianites, Ammonites, and the Philistines. From time to time, courageous men (and one courageous woman) stood up among the Israelites to rally the people and lead them against the enemies. Among the leaders, who became known as the Judges, were Deborah, Gideon, Jeptha, and Samson. The last and most famous Judge was the "seer," Samuel. He brought a spirit of unity among the people by strengthening their faith and uniting them in the worship of one God.

The period of Judges was followed by that of a new type of leaders, the Kings.

The period of Judges was followed by that of a new type of leaders, the Kings:

Saul. Towards the end of Samuel's period of office, he was persuaded by the people to place a king over them. The choice fell on Saul. At first successful, he later became estranged from Samuel. Saul was finally vanquished by the Philistines and David became the second king of Israel.

David. David was the greatest of Israel's kings. He brought the tribes into a firm union, took Jerusalem from the Jebusites and established it as his capital. He was successful on the battle field and, besides being a great ruler, David is the author of a large number of the Psalms. He left an empire to his son and successor, Solomon.

Solomon. 970 B.C.E. One of Solomon's first tasks was to build the magnificent Temple of God on Mount Zion. Most of his reign was characterized by peace and prosperity, reaping the profits of his father's greatness. Although traditionally he is seen as a wise man, he committed a grave political error in his foreign alliances, resulting in the introduction of idol worship into the Israelite kingdom. Also, in order to finance his extensive and luxurious buildings, the people were severely taxed.

On the death of Solomon the spirit of enmity that already existed between north and south, was brought to a climax through the heavier taxation by Solomon's heir. The kingdom was divided into two parts: the Kingdom of Israel in the north, with ten of the twelve tribes; and the Kingdom of Judah in the south, with the tribes of Judah and Benjamin, who remained loyal to the dynasty of David. The two kingdoms were bitter rivals and enemies. In addition, religious, social and political corruption were rampant in both kingdoms, creating a growing class of impoverished people in both countries.

To fight against the prevalent evil, the prophets fearlessly preached the message of truth. Elijah, Elisha, Amos, Hosea, Isaiah, Micah, and Jeremiah are among the immortal teachers of this period. Their strong message with its underlying spiritual force has been one of the greatest Jewish contributions to the world.

To fight against the prevalent evil, the prophets fearlessly preached the message of truth. Their strong message with its underlying spiritual force has been one of the greatest Jewish contributions to the world.

This period saw the rise of the great empires of Syria, Assyria, and Babylon. The northern kingdom of Israel succumbed before the might of Assyria in 721 B.C.E. and the ten tribes were dispersed. The kingdom of Judah continued for about a century and a half, and then fell under the great military power of Babylon in 586 B.C.E. The Temple was in ruins and the better part of the nation was exiled to Babylon. The longer existence of the kingdom of Judah is what gave Jews their final name. Judah in Hebrew is pronounced as "*Yehudah*," which led to the word "*Yehudi*" for those belonging to the kingdom. Today the Hebrew word for Jew still is "*Yehudi*."

The Second Jewish Commonwealth: 530 B.C.E.-70 C.E.

The exiles in Babylon settled down, mourning for Zion. But in 539 B.C.E., Cyrus of Persia overthrew the Babylonian empire and allowed those who wanted, to return to their native soil. The returning exiles overcame many obstacles, reconstructed their national life and built a new Temple. However, the small community lacked strong leadership and economic resources, and soon floundered.

Ezra the scribe, and later Nehemiah, joined the returned exiles and, due to their efforts, the people were molded into a strong community once more, devoted to the service of their God. Ezra was responsible for the religious revival of his people, while Nehemiah worked at strengthening the cities to withstand attack. The reforms of Ezra and Nehemiah introduced a long period of peace and quiet. Hardly affected by the comings and goings of great empires, the Jews organized themselves around their synagogues and settled down to a period of literary activity which is regarded as one of the most formative in Jewish history.

Peace was disturbed with the appearance of a new world conqueror, and Judea had to submit itself to the rule of Alexander the Great. Rich and opportunistic Hebrews abandoned their own civilization for what they considered the brighter and more profitable way of life of the Greeks.

Rich and opportunistic Hebrews abandoned their own civilization for what they considered the brighter and more profitable way of life of the Greeks.

After Alexander's death, the tiny Jewish state was the prize in a century of war between rival Syrian and Egyptian generals, until it finally came under rule of Antiochus of Syria.

Antiochus IV, striving to make his empire totally Greek and subservient, attempted to force a heathen religion upon the Jews, which led to the first recorded struggle for religious freedom. Led by the famous Maccabees, the Jews revolted and waged guerrilla warfare against an enemy stronger than their own ill-armed, ill-trained band. The fight against Antiochus was also something of a civil war, for the Hellenistic cult had made great inroads into Jewish life and there was bitter strife between the Hellenists and the "Pietists."

After a long struggle, the forces of Antiochus were defeated in 165 B.C.E. Later, around 140 B.C.E., the sole survivor of the Maccabean brothers, Simon, was made both High Priest and King of the nation. The rule of the Maccabees continued for about a century. Rome, the supreme power of the time, recognized the independence of Judea. But in 63 B.C.E., Pompeii intervened in a struggle for the throne and brought the country into submission to all-powerful Rome.

The Zealots of Galilee dreamed of independence, the Essenes dreamed of a world beyond, the nobles curried favor with the Roman rulers, while the Pharisees sought to keep the religion alive.

The Jews did not easily bear the Roman yoke. A succession of procurators vied with each other in their brutality towards the Jews, who were again divided. The Zealots of Galilee dreamed of independence, the Essenes dreamed of a world beyond, the nobles curried favor with the Roman rulers, while the Pharisees sought to keep the religion alive.

About this time a Jewish teacher by the name of Jesus of Nazareth began to influence some Jews, particularly in Galilee. Jesus did not teach rejection of the Torah. As a matter of fact, most of his ideas were good Jewish ethics. His disciples regarded him as the Messiah and he was accused by the Romans of being a menace to law and order. Jesus was crucified by the Romans, but his teaching was spread by his followers. Due mainly to Paul, the members of the new sect broke from Judaism and developed an entirely new religion.

The first war against Rome began about 66 C.E., when the Zealots organized open warfare against the rulers. The struggle was heroic but unequal, and in 70 C.E., Titus captured Jerusalem and burned the Temple. Thus ended the second Jewish State. Although Palestine remained the center of Jewish civilization for another two centuries, the number of Jews living outside the Holy Land actually exceeded those living in Israel.

The Period of the Rabbis: 70-200 C.E.

While the Romans were still besieging walls of Jerusalem, the farsighted action of Rabbi Jochanan ben Zakkai saved the center of Jewish learning from destruction. He laid the foundations of a new sort of life which was to keep the Jews as a distinctive entity. Without a Temple, without a land or independence and scattered throughout many widespread centers of Jewish presence, the Jews found their unifying principle in the Torah and its study.

For more than three centuries, the rabbinical Patriarchs were the recognized authorities of the Jewish world. It was a period of religious reconstruction and intense intellectual activity. The Synagogue and Prayer Book took the place of the Temple and sacrifices. Learning was widespread and religious education was made compulsory to a degree of almost universal literacy among the Jews.

The smoldering hatred against the Romans was easily stirred up. Taxes and refusal to permit Jerusalem to be rebuilt fanned the anger of the Jews into a roaring fire. The Jewish army rallied behind Bar Kochba in an attempt to overthrow the Romans once again. The heroic struggle received the support of Rabbi Akiva, the greatest teacher of the century, who proclaimed Bar Kochba as the Messiah.

Without a Temple, without a land or independence and scattered throughout many widespread centers of Jewish presence, the Jews found their unifying principle in the Torah and its study. The Synagogue and Prayer Book took the place of the Temple and sacrifices.

At first successful, the Jewish army soon had to face strong Roman forces, and one by one the Jewish strongholds of resistance were broken down. After the war, Emperor Hadrian imposed cruel restrictions on the Jewish community in Palestine, and many left their homeland. The successors of Hadrian lifted some of the laws and for a time the scholars of Palestine were left in comparative peace to continue the development of the Talmud.

In 200 C.E., Rabbi Judah the Prince, who lived in the Palestinian community, edited the Mishnah, *the great body of Oral Law developed by the rabbinical commentators.*

In 200 C.E., Rabbi Judah the Prince, who lived in the Palestinian community, edited the *Mishnah*, the great body of Oral Law developed by the rabbinical commentators. Yet in spite of his effort, the Palestinian community declined in importance. More important Talmudic studies were being carried out in Babylonia. Meanwhile, the rift between Judaism and Christianity grew wider and, when Christianity was adopted by Constantine as the official state religion (312 C.E.), the position of the Jews in Palestine grew intolerable, and Jewish leadership passed into the hands of the great scholars and rabbis of Babylonia.

The Diaspora:
From 200 to 1900 C.E.

The Jews in Babylon

Well before the destruction of the Temple in 70 C.E., Jews had already settled in Alexandria, Arabia, Asia Minor and on some of the Mediterranean islands. However, Babylonia became the most important center of Judaism, due to the exile. Jews possessed a large measure of autonomy there, and were exceedingly well organized. The Exilarch, or Prince of the Exile, was the recognized head of the people. The academies of Sura, Pumbeditha, Mehozah and Nehardea were overflowing and Jewish scholarship flourished. The great work of the Babylonian Talmud was completed about 500 C.E.

Babylonia became the most important center of Judaism, due to the exile.

The Talmud represents the record of the development of Jewish life and thought through the *Mishnah* and *Gemarah*, and its six orders cover every aspect of Jewish civilization. The Talmud, more than any other single factor, has been the most formative influence on Jewish life throughout history.

In post-Talmudic years the heads of schools were called *Geonim*, who not only carried religious authority for the Jews in Babylon, but outside Babylon as well. Their knowledge and wisdom was so highly regarded that they were recognized by Jews all over the Diaspora as their religious guides.

The Talmud, more than any other single factor, has been the most formative influence on Jewish life throughout history.

After 622 C.E., the Mohammedans began to sweep through the Byzantine empire, taking Palestine and conquering Persian ruled Babylon. At first the Mohammedans' rule was that of "The Koran or the Sword," but over time, fanatical zeal was tempered. They became satisfied with the tribute and homage of unbelievers.

By this time, Jewish life in Babylon was fast declining and the great splendor of Exilarch and *Geonim* became but a mere shadow. The rift caused by the Karaite sect — opponents of rabbinic authority — hastened Babylon's decline as the most important Jewish settlement. The academies and *Geonim* ceased to function in 1038 C.E. Another country had established itself as the center of Jewish life.

The Golden Age of Spanish Jewry: 900-1200 C.E.

In 711, the Arabs crossed the straits of Gibraltar and conquered Spain. For the next four centuries, Spain was the one bright star in a Europe darkened by the shadows of Christian persecution. The Moors and the Jews had much in common and, in the more or less peaceful atmosphere that prevailed, great Jewish philosophers, poets, statesmen and scientists created the most brilliant episode in the annals of Diaspora history. Among them were Chasdai ibn Shaprut, a physician and statesman who established correspondence with the Khazars, a people who converted to Judaism; Samuel the Prince, a poet and Talmud scholar; Solomon ibn Gabirol, a poet and philosopher of note, whose writings were studied far and wide and whose poems are still included in prayer books; Bachya ibn Pakuda, a philosopher and important writer on Jewish ethics; and Yehuda haLevi, one of the greatest Jewish poets, singer of love for Zion, with poems still read today. And probably the best known of all: Moses Maimonides, philosopher, physician and Talmudic scholar.

Moslem rule over Spain was whittled away by the Christians, who conquered all of Spain by the end of the 14th century, with the exception of Granada. It was the beginning of the end for the Spanish Jews, as persecution mounted. Destruction of property, forced baptism and death were the Jewish lot of the times. Under the leadership of the fanatic arch-inquisitor Torquemada the Inquisition rose to its highest point of efficiency. Its fury was directed mainly at the Marranos, or secret Jews, who outwardly professed Catholicism, but quietly kept the traditions of their ancestors in the seclusion of their homes. Torquemada was intent on driving out all Jews from Spain, and despite the plea of the noble Jewish statesman Abarbanel, the rulers of Spain followed the advice of the arch-inquisitor.

About 200,000 Jews were driven from the shores of Spain on August 2, 1492. When Christopher Columbus set out over the unchartered Atlantic, he saw many of the ships with the Jewish refugees in the harbor, ready to sail to any land that would accept them.

The Moors and the Jews had much in common and, in the more or less peaceful atmosphere that prevailed, great Jewish philosophers, poets, statesmen and scientists created the most brilliant episode in the annals of Diaspora history.

About 200,000 Jews were driven from the shores of Spain on August 2, 1492.

The Centuries of Medieval Europe: 1000-1700 C.E.

By the beginning of the 11th century, Jewish communities existed in most European countries. Unable to own land and barred from the guilds, Jews were driven to commerce and forced into money lending. Success didn't open society, however. Even when a Jew was successful and managed to exercise a considerable influence in finance he was still despised.

In cultural affairs the Jews devoted themselves to the study of their sacred books, especially the Talmud, and avoided any attempt to widen their intellectual interests in non-Jewish matters. The Jews became a strange element, the only non-Christians in Christian societies, forced to live differently from their neighbors. They moved about from one state to another, and were subjected to brutal treatment by their oppressors.

The misery of the Jews reached new lows during the period of the Crusades. In 1096, the first Crusade set out to regain Palestine from the Moslems. On their way, the Crusaders attacked the Jewish "enemies of the Church." When faced with the choice – baptism or death – whole Jewish communities perished. Every Crusade brought the same to the Jews, and those who survived were subjected to numerous restrictive and degrading laws.

These days of persecution rekindled interest in mysticism, which had always been (and still is) a strain of Jewish thought. In the 14th and 15th centuries in particular, the mysticism of the *Kabbala* seized the imagination of many Jews. Coupled with the great yearning for freedom, it led to the appearance of a group of false Messiahs. They claimed to be the leaders appointed by God who would bring an end to the suffering of the Jews and lead the nation back to Palestine. The most renowned of them all was Sabbatai Zevi, who lived between 1640 and 1670. He attracted a large following, as people were thirsting for a ray of hope to relieve the darkness of their lives. Great was their disappointment when the supposed messiah turned out to have no magical powers and at the end of his life even converted to Islam.

By the beginning of the 11th century, Jewish communities existed in most European countries.

The misery of the Jews reached new lows during the period of the Crusades.

Life in Old Poland and Russia: 1500-1900 C.E.

By the middle of the 16th century, Poland had become the largest and most important Jewish community.

By the middle of the 16th century, Poland had become the largest and most important Jewish community. The Jews were treated kindly by the kings and allowed to practice any trade and even operate farms. In turn, the Jews provided a much needed middle class for the Polish economy, which ensured them the protection of the rulers of the country. The Jews achieved a large measure of autonomy. Each community elected representatives to be members of the supreme Jewish "Council of the Four Lands." This Council met to decide on all matters affecting Jewish life in Poland: religious, legal, civil and particularly educational.

This peaceful period was brought to an end when the Greek-Orthodox Cossacks, ruled by the Roman Catholics of Poland, attacked the lords and nobles of the land. They vented their fury on the Jews, whom they considered to be the tools of the land-owning classes. A very large number of Jews lost their lives and a period of intense persecution began. It was after this event that many turned to the false messiahs like Sabbatai Zevi.

The Talmud states that without bread there can't be Torah. The often deadly poverty of the Jews led to a decline of literacy; there was no time to study for the poorest of the poor, every minute was needed to survive. A "revolution" led by Israel Baal Shem against the academic bookishness of Talmudic Judaism became known as Hassidism. The Baal Shem shifted the emphasis from scholarship to piety, from intellectual knowledge to emotional expression, from the Talmud to the Prayer Book. He preached that one must serve God in joy. This new message opened up a wonderful source of life for the masses, who sought to approach their God in new ways. The movement introduced a spirit of freshness and joy, of faith and a promise of a new life. Hassidism captured the imagination of Polish Jewry and did much to strengthen their religious identity.

The Baal Shem shifted the emphasis from scholarship to piety, from intellectual knowledge to emotional expression, from the Talmud to the Prayer Book.

Between 1772 and 1796, the state of chaos in Poland made possible that large parts of Polish territory were annexed by its neighbors. Russia took White Russia and the Ukraine, together with the more than one million Jews who lived there. At first, the Russian rulers tried to prevent the Jews from entering Russia territory. Later, they tried to Russianize the Jews. To accelerate this process, Nicholas I introduced "catchers" to kidnap an annual quota of Jewish youngsters for the army. Once enlisted they were cruelly treated in an attempt to force them to accept baptism.

Under Alexander II, reform and liberalism were introduced and the Jews were allowed some measure of freedom. But immediately after his assassination in 1881, a period of extreme reaction set in. Constant pogroms made life so intolerable that large numbers left Russia when America opened its doors to settlers in the 1880s to 1900s. Others began to plan for a new life in Palestine.

During the latter half of the 19th century, Russian Jewry witnessed the emergence of a new philosophy of enlightened interest in European culture, termed *"Haskalah."* The new movement originated in Germany and quickly spread to the other great centers of Jewish life. Young Talmud students began to take up the study of European culture and introduced an approach to Jewish subjects based on the scientific method.

Even before the French Revolution broke down the walls of the ghetto, the Jews of Germany were already picking away at them from within. Moses Mendelssohn was one of the foremost leaders of the Enlightenment. He worked for the emancipation of his people by introducing them to European culture.

When Liberty and Equality spread throughout Europe, the Jews were granted equal rights in countries conquered by Napoleon. In many cases it didn't take long for them to pay the price of emancipation, the price of complete assimilation. Large numbers of Jews, particularly in Germany, found their way to the baptismal font, most of them motivated by a desire to be accepted by the educated class of Christian society, which still looked down on Jews. Among the converts were members of the family of Moses Mendelssohn and the great poet Heine.

Slowly the Jews in Central Europe made their way into public life. In all countries — England, France, Germany — a stream of Jews entered occupations and professions which until then had been denied to them. Many illustrious Jews rose to positions of great eminence as statesmen, musicians and philanthropists in all communities.

Parallel to this was the emergence of Reform Judaism, which had its birth in Germany but proved to be a power of great importance in Amer-

During the latter half of the 19th century, Russian Jewry witnessed the emergence of a new philosophy of enlightened interest in European culture, termed "Haskalah."

ica. Jews had arrived with the very earliest settlers. By 1914 there were over 2 million Jews in the United States, and in all spheres of American life Jews were among the first progressive pioneers. Their mentality demanded a progressive kind of Judaism that found its shape in the typically American variety of Reform Judaism.

Toward the end of the 19th century it became clear that emancipation hadn't improved the Jewish position. Political anti-Semitism raised its head in Europe. An example of the new anti-Semitism showed itself in the trial of the French Jew Alfred Dreyfus. It was during this trial that Theodore Herzl clearly recognized the crux of the Jewish problem. His book, *The Jewish State*, was the result. With the first Zionist Congress of 1897 and the launching of the Zionist movement, began the most hopeful development in Jewish life. To many, Zionism seemed the one answer to the twofold problem of assimilation and attack.

From Horror to Liberation:
The Twentieth Century

The Early Struggles of Zionism

Some years before Herzl, many writers and thinkers had advocated that the salvation of the Jew depended on his return to Palestine. The *Chovevel Zion* movement had taken modest steps to further this aim. However, Herzl approached this task in a much more ambitious and urgent frame of mind. He spent himself in an attempt to secure an official charter which would secure Palestine as a Jewish State.

After his death, his successors continued the struggle. In the meantime, Jews bought and created new settlements, villages and towns in Palestine. Even the Hebrew language was revived. There had always been Jews in Palestine, but now a new spirit began to stir in the land.

Some years before Herzl, many writers and thinkers had advocated that the salvation of the Jew depended on his return to Palestine.

The Growth of Zionism

The Balfour Declaration of 1917 gave a new impulse to the Jews who longed to rebuild the country. Successive *aliyot* brought thousands of immigrants who wanted to create the miracle of a new nation by the name of Israel. In reaction, Arab opposition grew, which led to increasing and more complicated difficulties.

The first World War brought renewed suffering to the Jews of Eastern Europe. Many Jews found a place for themselves in the New Russia after the Revolution of 1917, but large numbers encountered great hardships during the civil war that followed. Many thousands fled from Eastern Europe to the United States, Canada, Argentina, and Brazil.

It seemed as if Europe didn't care about the drain of its Jewish population. After the first World War, European countries signed treaties granting ordinary rights to minority populations. Yet the social status and economic position of the Jews hardly improved.

The Balfour Declaration of 1917 gave a new impulse to the Jews who longed to rebuild the country.

The National-Socialist Party under Hitler declared the elimination of the Jews as its policy.

In Germany after World War I, the opponents of the democratic regime adopted a vicious anti-Semitic platform and demanded that Germany rid itself of its Jews altogether. The National-Socialist Party under Hitler declared the elimination of the Jews as its policy. The catastrophe that befell European Jewry in the second World War of 1939-1945 is unparalleled in the history of any other nation. The Nazis were responsible for the death of about six million Jews, which represented one-third of the Jewish world population at that time. Hundreds of thousands of people were shot, hundreds of thousands died of starvation and disease and more than 2 million perished in gas chambers which the Germans had established to carry out the "final solution to the Jewish problem." More than one million of those who were killed were children under the age of 13.

In other parts of the world – England and America – the Jews were comparatively free from violence, although non-governmental anti-Semitism remained a potential source of danger.

In other parts of the world – England and America – the Jews were comparatively free from violence, although non-governmental anti-Semitism remained a potential source of danger. Unfortunately, the attitude in those countries towards Jews was not favorable enough to open the gates of emigration for the Jews from the "slaughterhouse" that Europe had become.

The British, in spite of their promise to develop Palestine as a homeland for the Jewish people, bowed to Arab pressure and let their oil interests prevail, closing Palestine to Jewish immigrants during the few years before the war when hundreds of thousands could have escaped Europe. In addition, little or nothing was done to take advantage of several opportunities that could have saved ten of thousands of children.

It was this experience, more than any other, that accounts for the strong dedication and commitment of all Jews today to the preservation of the State of Israel. It is the only place in the world that can serve as a Jewish homeland and only Israel guarantees a refuge to all Jews.

After the second World War, the Jews were more determined than ever to establish a Jewish State in Palestine. The insurmountable difficulties of the Jewish-Arab conflict were earnestly discussed by the United Nations, which finally voted on November 29, 1947, to have an independent Jewish State set up in Palestine. The fact that it was 1947, just fifty years after the Zionist Congress at Basel in 1897, is rather interesting, because Theodore Herzl wrote the following in his diary just after attending the Congress:

"If I were to sum up the Congress in a work — which I shall take care not to publish — it would be this: At Basel I founded the Jewish State. If I said this out loud today I would be greeted by universal laughter. In five years, perhaps, and certainly in 50 years everyone will perceive it."

When Great Britain relinquished its mandate over the country in May 1948, the Jews declared the establishment of an independent State of Israel. Seven Arab States immediately attacked, but the Jews successfully withstood the powerful dominance. Within eight years of its existence as an independent state, Israel more than doubled its Jewish population by mass immigration of Jews from 70 communities all over the world. Unfortunately, the hostility and hatred of the Arabs toward Israel remained. Russian interference and the failing of internal reforms in their own countries made the leaders of the Arab states more and more violent towards Israel. Organized bands of terrorists constantly crossed Israel's borders, and Syrian artillery frequently shelled Israel's farming villages.

In May of 1967, the Egyptians ordered the United Nations Emergency Force, which had controlled the border of the Gaza Strip and the area of the Straits of Tiran, to leave Egypt. 80,000 Egyptian soldiers moved to the border and President Gamel Nasser announced that the Straits of Titan would be closed to Israeli shipping.

The United Nations and Western diplomacy failed to reopen the Straits of Tiran. Syria and Jordan moved troops and equipment into position and ringed Israel. When the threats of Arab leaders to wipe out the Jews became more strident, Israel decided to mobilize its defense forces. War broke out on June 5, 1967: a country of fewer than 2,500,000 against an Arab world of 70,000,000. A land of 8,000 square miles against close to 3,000,000 square miles. In six days the Israeli defense forces defeated the Arab armies that surrounded Israel. As a result of the war, Jerusalem was reunified.

The State of Israel had announced that it wanted no sons of other lands to fight for it. Yet thousands of Jewish volunteers, and many non-Jews, came to Israel before and after the fighting in order to help. Since Israel had very little of a standing army and most of the Israelis were at the front, volunteers were very much welcome to keep civilian services running.

War broke out on June 5, 1967: a country of fewer than 2,500,000 against an Arab world of 70,000,000. In six days the Israeli defense forces defeated the Arab armies that surrounded Israel. As a result of the war, Jerusalem was reunified.

Following the Six Days' War the position of the Jewish minority in the Soviet Union, probably over 2,500,000, became worse. From its low point under the rule of the Czar, the circumstances had improved somewhat for the Jews during the early decades of Communist rule, but underwent steady deterioration under the regime of Stalin and his successors. Jews were accused of plotting to poison Soviet leaders, and were frequently accused of being Zionist or capitalist stooges, or agents for the CIA. While other minority groups were allowed to maintain their culture, Jews were not allowed to teach Hebrew or to have Jewish schools, newspapers and theaters. As a faith, Judaism was subjected to the same restrictions as other religious groups in Russia.

Since the collapse of Communism, Jewish self-awareness has increased dramatically in Eastern Europe.

Since the collapse of Communism, Jewish self-awareness has increased dramatically in Eastern Europe: we find the resurrection of synagogues, the creation of Jewish schools for children as well as adults, Jewish summer camps and a myriad of other Jewish institutions. At the same time, Israel has experienced an overwhelming immigration from the former Warsaw Pact countries. Not only has Russian immigration to Israel been significant, but so have *aliyot* from Latin America. It could be argued that these two groups have economical motives to move to Israel, while among Americans and immigrants from other wealthy countries ideological motives prevail. Whatever the individual considerations for leaving everything one knows for Israel, it shows that Israel is still fulfilling the Zionist ideal of being a haven of refuge and safety for all Jews who seek a better life. Both these new and the old Israelis have one common experience and one shared ideal: They all participate in the slow but steady struggle for peace with all of Israel's neighbors, which until now has resulted in peace agreements with Egypt and Jordan.

The American Jewish Community

An Historical View

The American Jewish community got its start in the United States in 1654, when 23 Jews landed in New Amsterdam. They had come from Brazil, which they had to leave when Portugal recaptured it and closed the colony to all but Roman Catholics. Between then and the American Revolution a few thousand Jews found their way to the United States. They formed congregations in Savannah, Newport, Philadelphia, Charleston and New York City.

From about 1816-1820 to the time of the Civil War, but especially after the Revolution of 1848 in Germany, a substantial number of German Jews flocked to the United States. These Jews settled largely in the South and Midwest, most of them peddlers and working their way up to merchants and tradesmen in the small towns and cities of the frontier. A few of these peddlers went on to found some of the great department stores that still exist today.

It was during this time that the first Rabbis came to the United States. Some of them were Reform Rabbis who began to introduce changes in the previously Orthodox synagogues and by the 1850s and 60s several of the German congregations had become Reform. In 1875 Isaac Mayer Wise established Hebrew Union College as the first Rabbinical Seminary in the New World. At that time there were about 270 congregations and 230,000 Jews in the United States.

Between 1881 and 1914, pogroms and persecutions sparked the third mass movement to America of predominantly Eastern European Jews. The majority of them settled in New York and other major cities along the East Coast. The immigrants from Eastern Europe crossed the Atlantic from a backward economy and entered into the middle of a rapidly expanding, highly mobile, individualistic society.

This first generation worked hard in America both to make a living and to enable their children to get that much prized Jewish object, an

The American Jewish community got its start in the United States in 1654, when 23 Jews landed in New Amsterdam.

Between 1881 and 1914, pogroms and persecutions sparked the third mass movement to America of predominantly Eastern European Jews.

education. The emphasis in Jewish tradition on education and family solidarity, and the willingness of Jews to work hard, led to a rapid rise in the economic level of the Jewish community. In less than two generations, the immigrants who had lived in crowded conditions in the tenements and slums of the major cities produced professionals, businessmen, craftsmen, and creative artists in abundance.

The second generation, however, nurtured in American public schools and growing up with American values, came into conflict with the strongly Yiddish Orthodox, Eastern European ways of their parents. Many Jews of the second generation abandoned Orthodox Judaism, and since they knew no Jewish alternative to the Orthodoxy they grew up with, they became secular or ethnic Jews. They still felt a strong identity with the Jewish people and its history but without ties to the synagogue.

The rise of the third and fourth generations of American Jews in the period following World War II produced a new set of circumstances. These people no longer felt embarrassment for the immigrant Yiddish culture of their parents and grandparents and they set about to create a Jewish identity for themselves compatible with American life and culture. In this period of the 1940s to the 1960s, there was a substantial rise in the number of congregations in the Reform and Conservative branches of Judaism.

There was also a rise in Jewish education on all levels. In 1940 there were 35 Jewish all day schools with 7,700 students. By 1950 this had increased to 139 schools with 23,100 students and in 1960 it was 265 schools with 55,800 students. 90% of these Jewish day schools were Orthodox. Another major development in Jewish educational activity was the rise in Jewish summer camps maintained by religious or Zionist organizations. While most of the summer camps catered to children, many were used for adult groups with programs featuring study and discussion groups, services and creative projects related to Jewish tradition.

The View from Within

While its piety and scholarship is below that of previous historic Jewish communities, the American Jewish community does excel in the areas of *tsedakah* (philanthropy), an important Jewish *mitzvah.* There are literally hundreds of Jewish organizations that have philanthropic purposes. In fact, the Jews were pioneers in the establishment of United Fund-type campaigns. Every city has its United Jewish Welfare Fund or Allied Jewish Appeal campaigns. The American Jewish community raised 148 million dollars in 1948 under the impact of the miracle of the birth of the State of Israel. In 1967 that earlier amount was surpassed for the first time as American Jews once again rallied to support Israel's fight for survival.

Jews have for a long time pooled their resources to help those in need within their community. From Biblical times, Jews have been taught that a central feature of the religion was to care for the poor and needy. In early medieval times, synagogues collected funds to help the hungry and the homeless, and communities even raised money to redeem members who were sold into slavery. When there was a need for orphanages, the community built them. When Jewish hospitals were needed where people could be treated and observe their religion, Jewish societies set up and equipped such hospitals. Today, the federal and state governments provide various welfare services that the Jews used to offer within the Jewish community. This does not mean that the raising of money in the Jewish community has decreased. New needs are always arising and the Jews respond by contributing a portion of their income for the services they deem important. The fact of giving is looked upon as a *mitzvah*, a religious act.

Another characteristic of the American Jewish community has been its active interest in seeking to abolish slums, to help minorities (especially African Americans) to achieve civil rights, and to protect the rights and freedoms of all individuals. Jews were involved in the civil right movement from an early time and were among the founders of the NAACP. They also participated in the freedom rides and the sit-ins in the South. The Jews, more than any other group, whether defined by religion, economic background, or education, opposed the wild attacks upon individuals' patriotism by Senator McCarthy and others during the early fifties, when people were worked up about communist subversion. Although the Jewish community, by and large, is middle class, it nevertheless continues to identify more with the underdog and with the disadvantaged than with the complacent establishment.

Jews have for a long time pooled their resources to help those in need within their community.

Another characteristic of the American Jewish community has been its active interest in seeking to abolish slums, to help minorities (especially African Americans) to achieve civil rights, and to protect the rights and freedoms of all individuals.

The American Jewish community is slowly establishing its own cultural pattern.

The American Jewish community is slowly establishing its own cultural pattern. Whereas the Babylonian community developed the Talmud, the Spanish community concentrated on poetry and philosophy, and the Eastern European community devoted itself to the study of commentaries on the Talmud, the American Jewish community seems to be making its mark in the area of the novel and drama. Since World War II, not a year has passed without a best-seller on a Jewish subject or by a Jewish author, and Jewish playwrights are turning increasingly to Jewish themes.

The *mitzvah* of the study of Torah is not limited solely to the Bible in the Jewish tradition. Jewish tradition and teachings can be authentically expressed, and studied, in the form of literature. This does not mean that every work written by a Jew is Jewish in philosophy, emotion or concept. But when it is, it becomes a meaningful expression of Judaism, even when it is critical of Jewish life (after all, who were more critical than the Prophets?), as long as the author is sincerely devoted to the fate of the people of Israel.

Jewish Life Options: The Main Jewish Movements Today

Although we use words like "movements" or "currents," to be more in agreement with the Jewish spirit it is preferable to think in terms of "approaches to Judaism." No approach has more value than another, nor is it more "correct" or more "Jewish." Each approach reflects the different ways that today's Jewry lives and conceives its Judaism.

It is also worth remembering that, until Emancipation, these "movements" did not exist. The differences between groups was determined more by geographical difference, especially and most notably between *Sefardim* and *Ashkenazim*, but also within those groups or between those groups and others, such as the Italian or Ethiopian Jews.

Furthermore, there has always been a great diversity in different schools of thought and interpretation. Although two Orthodox Jews might look identical to the outsider, subtle differences in appearance can reveal fundamental differences in explanation and experience of Judaism.

The three largest movements of contemporary Judaism are the Orthodox, the Reform (or progressive, or liberal), and the Conservative. We will also review other minority currents such as Hassidism, Reconstructionism, and Humanistic Judaism.

Outside of the United States and Israel, where these denominations are less specific and formal, the breakdown is usually between the Orthodox and non-Orthodox blocks. In Europe, for instance, the equivalent of the American Conservative movement is called both "Reform" and "*Masorti*," while in America there are significant differences between these two denominations. 65% of all the synagogues in the world are non-Orthodox.

The Orthodox Movement

The denomination "Orthodox" is relatively recent and came from the opposition to the changes introduced by the *Haskalah* (the Jewish Enlight-

Although we use words like "movements" or "currents," to be more in agreement with the Jewish spirit it is preferable to think in terms of "approaches to Judaism." Furthermore, there has always been a great diversity in different schools of thought and interpretation.

Of all the movements, the Orthodox is the least centralized and the most diverse.

Orthodox theology sustains that the Torah, both the written and the "oral" (Talmud), were dictated letter by letter and word by word by God to Moses, without any kind of human "interference."

enment from 1700 to 1800, which would later produce the Reform movement and Zionism). Of all the movements, the Orthodox is the least centralized and the most diverse. It is better to speak of many movements and tendencies that share a series of common beliefs relating to the strict observance of Jewish Law (*Halacha*), Torah study, and the performance of the 613 precepts (*mitzvot*). But, at the same time, the different Orthodox tendencies have very different (at times even opposite) ways of understanding the Jewish relationship with contemporary society.

Orthodox theology sustains that the Torah, both the written and the "oral" (Talmud), were dictated letter by letter and word by word by God to Moses, without any kind of human "interference." In the light of the challenges of the modern world, Orthodox Jews propose the path of *Halacha* as the only way for a Jew to live. Daily life of an Orthodox Jew is governed by the fulfillment of the *mitzvot*. The Orthodox maintain many ancient practices regarding relationships, marriage, and divorce, and the interaction between the sexes in general. For instance, in Orthodox synagogues men and women are still separated.

Some Orthodox movements avoid any contact with the secular world, both Jewish and non-Jewish. There are Zionist Orthodox movements, like the *Mizrahi* in Israel. But then there is also a strand of Orthodoxy which fiercely opposes the State of Israel because it wasn't created by the Messiah.

In the U.S., the Orthodox community makes up only about 7% of the Jewish population. This percentage increases considerably in Europe and especially in Israel, where the non-Orthodox movements are small and very limited, due primarily to the political power wielded by the Orthodox rabbis.

It is interesting to point out that the reaction to the *Haskalah* (which, as has been stated, is the starting point of the three main movements) arose from the intellectual debates in Central Europe in the 18th and 19th centuries, so this division affects only the Ashkenazic world. The Sefardic communities in the Arab countries, where there was no "rationalist" movement either within the Jewish world or in the secular world, were therefore outside of this debate altogether and even today the *Sefardim* are synonymous with tradition and orthodoxy.

The Reform Movement

The Reform movement is a direct result of Europe's period of Enlightenment in the 18th century. The introduction of rationality as the primary source of knowledge found its way into Judaism by the name of *Haskalah*. The protagonist of the fusion of Jewish tradition and modern thinking was Moses Mendelssohn. Born in 1729 in Dessau, Germany, as the son of a poor Torah scribe, he received a good traditional Jewish education and became a brilliant Talmud student. Yet at the same time he broadened the scope of his studies to disciplines which were unheard of for a yeshiva student: French, Italian, English, Latin, Greek, Mathematics, Logic, and Philosophy.

The religious philosophy of Mendelssohn, influenced by and containing strong intersections with that of Wolff, Leibniz, and Spinoza, conceives God as a perfect Being. He argued that belief in God does not depend on such a belief. As a rationalist, he stated that Revelation did not contradict Reason or, to say it differently: one could rationally discover the reality of God, Divine Providence, and the immortality of the soul.

In 1783 Mendelssohn published *Jerusalem, or on Religious Power and Judaism*. It states that no religious institution can use coercion and excommunication against its dissidents, as had occurred with Spinoza. According to Mendelssohn, this notion of freedom of thought applied especially to Judaism, which has no dogmas. Any man or woman can rationally reach the philosophical truths of religion, with Judaism offering a unique path to these philosophical truths through its revealed moral code, its rituals, and its morality.

Mendelssohn wanted to integrate the Jews in the new civil societies, believing that Jews should make their own "social contract" with the Gentile societies in which they lived. In the atmosphere of 19th-century Europe, the philosophy of Mendelssohn developed beyond the realm of "ideas." When Napoleon gave legal equality to Jews, many finally had access to new positions and jobs which were previously prohibited. However, when Napoleon was defeated and his legislation was annulled, for many Jews the only way to maintain their recently attained positions was conversion to Christianity.

According to Mendelssohn, this notion of freedom of thought applied especially to Judaism, which has no dogmas. Mendelssohn wanted to integrate the Jews in the new civil societies, believing that Jews should make their own "social contract" with the Gentile societies in which they lived.

Many rabbis realized that the only way to keep the Jews away from the "Christian path" was not to bring them back into the ghetto, but to favor the ways in which they could continue being Jews without removing themselves from secular society, with its universities and intellectual centers. Following this line of thought, it was Leopold Zunz who proposed that Jews should apply secular and rational methods to study their own history.

This brought an immediate and radical changes in religious services, with the goal of making them better understood and more familiar. Mixed seating for men and women and the use of the German vernacular were only two of the changes. This initial "German Reform" movement was much more extreme than it is today and had a series of distinctive characteristics, rejecting many traditional practices because it considered them "barbaric." It eliminated, for example, circumcision and the idea of the reestablishment of the State of Israel in favor of making Germany a new Zion. It substituted the *Bar Mitzvah* ceremony with Confirmation. And it declared the dietary laws of *kashrut* and purity laws simply "disgusting to modern thought." Of course, all of this was blasphemy in the eyes of the Orthodox authorities, who fiercely and sometimes violently opposed the Reform movement, even going so far as appealing to the governments in order to close the centers of Reform Judaism.

Although the first Reform communities were created in Germany between 1810 and 1820 (Seesen, Hamburg, and Berlin), it was in the United States of the 19th century that the movement grew and became a real entity. Jewish immigrants from Germany transformed their Reform movement into the American Jewish movement par excellence in America, with 90% of all synagogues being Reform.

In 1855, the first major meeting of American rabbis took place. It was then that the theology and principles of the Reform movement were defined in a document known as the Pittsburgh Platform. The Platform abolished all laws and customs that were considered outdated and didn't show any adaptation to contemporary life. Instead, Jews should accept only those practices that helped to "elevate and sanctify our lives." In 1875, Rabbi Isaac Meyer Wise, the great architect of the Reform movement, created Hebrew Union College, where future Reform rabbis are still educated. Over the course of the following decades, the Reform movement questioned many of its initial reforms (this, after all, is one of the characteristics of the movement: continuous reform and revision). In the Columbus Platform of 1937, many practices once discarded were reinstated, and it inaugurated a process of renovation within the movement that continues until today, reflected in the platforms of San Francisco in 1976, Miami in 1997, and Pittsburgh in 1999.

The theology of the Reform movement is different in many ways from that of the Orthodox movement. The "Oral Law" of the Talmud is not considered "divine revelation," but is viewed as a series of reflections and ideas of thinkers that led several generations in their search for a path to God. After all, the Talmud is the summary of this search. It doesn't give clear answers to specific questions, but rather opinions that can lead to answers. According to Reform theology, the Jewish belief system is not dogmatic, but is instead the result of consensus, the result of what different contradictory opinions have in common.

The Reform movement believes that each generation has its own teachers and that venerating those of the past simply because they represent the past is a way of halting the tradition of logic and continuous adaptation that defines Judaism. When Reform Judaism analyzes a certain period in history, the premise is that the specific needs of the Jewish communities in that period led them to devise certain laws instead of others. Once those circumstances change, however, the formula may also cease to be valid.

Today's world is not the Palestine of the 1st century, or the Eastern Europe of the Middle Ages. So in light of a new situation, the Reform authorities consider rabbinical literature and *Halacha* (rabbinical law) as a huge depository of opinions and wisdom where one can sometimes find solutions, and sometimes not. In cases where there is no answer, we have to find our own answers, solutions, and responses. Judaism, for the Reform movement, is about diversity and personal freedom and autonomy, without any kind of sex discrimination or other distinctions. This contrasts with traditional, Orthodox Judaism that has chosen a specific path that perpetuates extant laws and that disregards and even oppresses alternative interpretations proposed by other rabbis.

The "Oral Law" of the Talmud is not considered "divine revelation," but is viewed as a series of reflections and ideas of thinkers that led several generations in their search for a path to God.

The Reform movement believes that each generation has its own teachers and that venerating those of the past simply because they represent the past is a way of halting the tradition of logic and continuous adaptation that defines Judaism.

Reform Judaism doesn't define itself as a 19th-century modern answer to traditional Judaism, but as a Judaism that is in constant transformation.

Although some of the original principles of "Classical Reform Judaism" reflect the times in which they were formulated, other principals still hold value in the present.

The Reform movement is the main current in the United States, with synagogues throughout the country and dozens of associations and organizations. The most important are the Central Conference of American Rabbis (CCAR) and the Union of American Hebrew Congregations (UAHC). The World Union for Progressive Judaism (WUPJ) supports and brings together the liberal communities outside of the United States.

Classical Reform Judaism

Reform Judaism doesn't define itself as a 19th-century modern answer to traditional Judaism, but as a Judaism that is in constant transformation. If those who were present in the beginning of Reform Judaism could see how it expresses itself today, they would hardly be able to recognize what they had started. Not only time has brought change, so has geography. Where non-American Reform Judaism (usually known as Liberal Judaism) has always been less radical in defining itself, the pioneers of Reform Judaism in America felt that the challenges of the New World should be met with the newest of ideas.

Today, there is still a small but significant group of congregations that retains the original ideas of America's earliest reformers. These congregations practice what has become known as "Classical Reform Judaism." Although some of the original principles of "Classical Reform Judaism" reflect the times in which they were formulated, like acceptance and conformity of the manners, dress and customs of America, other principals still hold value in the present: a rejection of religious laws that have no moral significance and are not applicable to modern life and complete adherence to the laws pertaining to morals and ethics; a style of worship that doesn't require ritual garments like *kippot* and *talliyot* to gain significance. It chooses English as its main language to create more understanding and meaning, it emphasizes the rabbi's sermon as moral guidance instead of Torah reading as the central part of services, and Confirmation is the celebration of coming of age as opposed to a *Bar* or *Bat Mitzvah* ceremony.

Although Classical Reform Judaism used to be mainstream Reform Judaism and has become a minority, the vibrancy of its congregations suggests that Classical Reform Judaism will always have a legitimate place within Reform Judaism. As mainstream Reform Judaism will always try to redefine itself, Classical Reform Judaism will always be the firm root of the blossoming tree.

The Conservative Movement

The Conservative movement is popularly seen as a moderate reform, a middle ground between the Orthodox and Reform movements. In terms of numbers, the Conservative movement makes up the second largest Jewish group in the world, only slightly surpassed by the Reform movement. The Conservative movement was created in the United States in 1913 when Solomon Schechter founded the United Synagogue of Conservative Judaism (USCJ). The name "Conservative" or "*Masorti*" came from the conviction that neither orthodoxy nor reformism would be capable of conserving and preserving Jewish life in a society like that of the United States.

Like the Reform movement, the Conservative movement argues that there has always been a continuous evolution of ideas and customs in Judaism, aimed at adapting to the changes at different times in different places. The radical differences between the two movements deal with the nature of Revelation and the observance of Jewish Law. While the Reform movement generally follows the approach of modern biblical criticism and views the Bible as the expression of several authors' ideas of the divine, Conservative Judaism considers that somehow the hand of God was present in the writing of the texts, although they admit that there was more than one writer and that the influence of other cultures was a factor operating in the sacred books. Accordingly, the Conservative movement sees *Halacha* as a product of the wishes of God. Solomon Schechter developed the concept of *Kahal* (the community of observant Jews), to justify the decisions on Jewish Law.

The Halachic authority of the Conservative movement is the Jewish Committee of Law and Standards, which in many occasions offers several solutions to one given topic, allowing each community to apply what is most useful to them. This leads to several different tendencies in the movement, depending on the role given to women and the weight of *Halacha*. The exception to this "local autonomy" of communities are the "standards," de-

While the Reform movement generally follows the approach of modern biblical criticism and views the Bible as the expression of several authors' ideas of the divine, Conservative Judaism considers that somehow the hand of God was present in the writing of the texts.

cisions voted by 80% of the members of the JCLS and the majority vote of the Rabbinical Assembly (RA). Today, there are four "standards," namely:

1. Rabbis and cantors cannot officiate or participate actively in mixed marriages.

2. Rabbis cannot officiate the second marriage of somebody who has not halachically divorced (*get*) his or her first spouse or whose marriage has not been annulled (*hafka'at Kidushin*) or is not a widow(er).

3. Matrilineal descent is the proper way to determine Jewish identity.

4. Conversions to Judaism that do not include the circumcision of males and the ritual immersion (*mikvah*) for men and women are not accepted.

In the Spanish-speaking world, the Conservative movement is the largest non-Orthodox force. To a large extent, this is due to the efforts of the *Seminario Rabínico Latinoamericano* in Argentina, founded by Rabbi Marshall T. Meyer and Rabbi Theodore Friedman. The most important organization of the Conservative Movement is the USCJ (United Synagogue of Conservative Judaism), and its seminary, the Jewish Theological Seminary (JTS).

Hassidism

Hassidism is an Orthodox movement, but with a series of peculiarities which differentiate it distinctly from the other Orthodox tendencies, such as their typical black clothing and a search for occult or mystical aspects of the Torah. It was founded in Eastern Europe in the 18th century by Rabbi Israel ben Eliezer, also known as the Baal Shem Tov, or BeSH ("He who possesses the Good Name" or "Teacher of the Divine Name"). His followers insisted that he was so close to God that by uttering God's names he could work miracles.

In the face of the traditional and dry intellectualism of Judaism, Hassidism proposed song and dance as forms of praise. It was a less rational way of religious life and provided a more emotional perspective that allowed every Jew to come closer to God in everything that he or she did. With its vitality, its joyfulness, and its search for mystical and deep aspects in the Torah, Hassidism rapidly extended throughout all of Eastern Europe, despite the harsh criticism of the Orthodox authorities.

In the face of the traditional and dry intellectualism of Judaism, Hassidism proposed song and dance as forms of praise.

With its vitality, its joyfulness, and its search for mystical and deep aspects in the Torah, Hassidism rapidly extended throughout all of Eastern Europe, despite the harsh criticism of the Orthodox authorities.

When the Baal Shem Tov died in 1760, the movement fragmented into many sub-currents and sects. Around 1830, the Hassidic impulse practically died out due to the new ideas derived from the *Haskalah*, Zionism and Socialism. The majority of Hassidic schools and centers that managed to survive modernization were completely destroyed by the Nazis during the Holocaust. However, the thought of authors such as Martin Buber and Abraham Joshua Heschel helped to prepare the path for the powerful resurgence of a new generation of Hassidic Jews which started around 1970. Presently, Hassidism is becoming one of the most solid groups of Orthodoxy.

There are several Hassidic movements today. The most well known is *Chabad Lubavitch*, with more than 100,000 followers throughout the world. After *Chabad*, the largest Hassidic movements are *Gor* (*Gerer*), *Viznitz*, and *Bealz* (*Belzer*), followed by others such as *Bobov, Bostoner, Satmar, Puppa, Bianer, Munkacz*, and *Rimnitz*.

Reconstructionism

Despite the small number of members (barely 1% of world Jewry), Reconstructionism tends to be seen as one of the main movements of contemporary Judaism. This preeminence is doubtlessly owed to the importance and respect given to its founder, Mordechai Kaplan (1881-1983), and his texts. Kaplan studied at the Jewish Theological Seminary in New York and for a brief period of time he was the rabbi of an Orthodox community. In 1922 he created the Society for the Advancement of Judaism, which in 1935 became the Foundation of Reconstructionist Judaism. In 1968 he created the Reconstructionist Rabbinical University in order to ordain that movement's rabbis.

Kaplan viewed Judaism as a civilization and God as a "power in the process of Salvation." Kaplan said that "we can no longer conceive God as a kind of invisible 'superman,' with the same psychological blueprints as human beings, but on a much larger scale. We cannot think of Him loving, feeling pity, rewarding, punishing..." Therefore, prayer is not directed to a "something;" it is something that makes us realize that we are part of a process and it benefits primarily us, as praying people, before transforming the circumstances of the world around us.

Kaplan viewed Judaism as a civilization and God as a "power in the process of Salvation." Prayer is not directed to a "something;" it is something that makes us realize that we are part of a process and it benefits primarily us, as praying people, before transforming the circumstances of the world around us.

Kaplan's theology has been misunderstood many times in the past (such as the idea that Kaplan was an agnostic). With regard to Revelation, for instance, the original Reconstructionist theology of Kaplan (now questioned by some of the movement's rabbis) argued that the Torah was not inspired by God, but rather is part of the Jewish people's folklore and, as such, it should be preserved, in order to guarantee the perpetuation of Jewish civilization.

Within Judaism itself Kaplan is probably best known as the creator of the *Bat Mitzvah*, the coming of age ceremony for girls. The first ceremony took place in 1922 with his own daughter, Judith, and was later adopted by the Reform movement and some branches of the Conservative movement.

The Reconstructionist movement is structured around the Reconstructionist Federation of Congregations and *Chavurot*.

Other movements

Humanistic Judaism, in existence since 1963, focuses on maintaining Jewish identity without the need to appeal to a belief in a personal God as creator and ruler of the world.

There are other minor, more contemporary movements that approach Judaism in different ways. Humanistic Judaism, in existence since 1963, focuses on maintaining Jewish identity without the need to appeal to a belief in a personal God as creator and ruler of the world; and embraces a human-centered philosophy that combines the celebration of Jewish culture and identity with an adherence to humanistic values and ideas.

Jewish Renewal is the youngest branch of Judaism. It is a pluralistic movement which explores traditional Kabbalistic and Hassidic theory and practice within a non-Orthodox framework, incorporating such liberal social phenomena as feminism, environmentalism and pacifism. Jewish Renewal adds to traditional worship ecstatic practices such as meditation, chant and dance and in seeking to reinvigorate Jewish ritual, Renewal Jews borrow freely and openly from Asian and Native American religions.

Timeline

B.C.E.:	Before the Common (or Christian) Era
C.E.:	Common (or Christian) Era

2000 B.C.E.	Abraham
1220	The Exodus from Egypt, under the leadership of Moses

The Period of the Judges

1150	Deborah, Gideon, Abimelech and others
1100-1020	Samuel

The First Kings of Israel

1028-1013	Saul reigns as King
1013-973	Reign of David as King
973-933	Reign of Solomon as King
960	Building of the First Temple by Solomon
933	Division of the Jewish Kingdom: Rehoboam, King of Judah; Jeroboam, King of Israel (the Northern Kingdom)
721	The fall of the Northern Kingdom; destroyed by the Assyrians. The last Ten Tribes
586	Fall of Judea, the Southern Kingdom. The destruction of the First Temple by the Babylonians. The beginning of the Babylonian Exile
538	Cyrus, the Persian ruler, gives permission to return to Palestine
516	The completion of the Second Temple
458	The second return to Judea under Ezra
445	Nehemiah, governor of Judea; Ezra reads the Law (Five books of Moses)
331	Alexander the Great passes through Judea. Jews of Palestine come under the rule and influence of the Greeks

285-247	The Bible translated into Greek
168	Antiochus IV, Syrian-Greek ruler over Palestine, forbids Jews to practice Judaism. Maccabees begin war of rebellion against Antiochus and his armies
165	The Temple rededicated
142	Judea becomes an independent State under the reign of the Maccabees
63	Pompey, the Roman ruler, enters Jerusalem
39-4 C.E.	Herod becomes King of Judea. Hillel, one of the greatest Rabbis, who created the *Mishnah*
66	War with Rome under Vespasian
70	Destruction of the Second Jewish State. Burning of the Second Temple by Titus on the 9th of *Av.* Dispersion of the Jews
90	Session of the *Sanhedrin* (the highest religious court) at Jabneh; Canonization of the Bible
132-135	Rebellion of Bar Kochba and Rabbi Akiva against Rome and its ruler Hadrian; defeat of the Rebellion
220	The *Mishnah* compiled, edited and written by Rabbi Judah The Prince, in Palestine
219-247	Rabbinic School founded at Sura in Babylon
500	Babylonian Talmud (*Mishnah* and *Gemara*) compiled and completed
740	Conversion of Khazars to Judaism
767	The revolt of the Karaites against the Talmud
892-942	Saadiah, Gaon of Sura and religious head of Babylonian Jews
1000	Marks beginning of the Jewish Golden Era in Spain (Moslem); Spain replaces Babylon as the center of Jewish learning
1021-1070	Solomon ibn Gabirol, the great Hebrew Poet and Philosopher (Spain)
1040-1105	Rashi (Rabbi Solomon ben Isaac) of France, the great commentator of the Bible and Talmud
1086-1142	Yehuda haLevi, the great Hebrew poet and religious thinker

AT-A-GLANCE

1135-1204	Moses Maimonides, a great philosopher and physician; the greatest authority on the Jewish law, author of the most important code of Law and the 13 Principles of Faith
1099	The Crusades; Capture of Jerusalem by Godfrey de Bouillon. Crusaders kill vast numbers of Jews and destroy many Jewish communities in France and Germany
1244	Burning of the Talmud in France
1290	Jews expelled from England
1348	Massacres of the Jews during the Black Plague
1333-1370	Casimir the Great invites Jews to Poland
1394	Jews expelled from France
1492	Jews expelled from Spain. Jewish community in Turkey emerges as one of the leading Jewish centers in the world
1654	First 23 Jews arrive in New Amsterdam (New York)
1648	Persecution of the Jews in Poland by the Cossacks
1656	Menasseh ben Israel appeals to Cromwell to readmit Jews to England, which occurs several years latter
1632-1677	Baruch Spinoza, the great philosopher who was excommunicated by the Jewish leaders of Amsterdam in 1656
1700-1760	Israel Baal Shem Tov, founder of the Hassidic Movement
1778	Moses Mendelssohn translates the Bible into German and helps German Jews emancipate themselves from the isolation of the ghetto
1791	Jews made citizens of France by the French National Assembly
1848	German Jews migrate to the United States
1881	Persecution of Jews in Russia and the beginning of a great migration of Jews from Russia and East European countries to the U.S. European Jews begin to colonize Palestine
1894	Dreyfus case in France
1897	August 29: First Zionist Congress with Herzl at Basel, marking the beginning of the Zionist Movement. The goal of Zionism to establish a Jewish State in Palestine wins the hearts of the Jewish masses of Europe

AT-A-GLANCE

1917	The Balfour Declaration issued by Great Britain which contained a pledge to help realize the Zionist Dream
1920	The League of Nations give Britain a mandate over Palestine
1943	Nazi leaders gain control over Germany and begin brutal treatment of the Jews
1939-1945	During Second World War, Nazis destroy 6 million Jews
1947	The United Nations vote Partition Plan for Palestine and set up a Jewish State
1948	Jewish leaders in Palestine declare the independence of the State of Israel
1956	Sinai War. Sinai and Gaza Strip occupied
1967	The Six Day War reunites Jerusalem under Israeli control. Israel occupies Golan Heights and Judea and Samaria
1968-70	Egypt's War of Attrition against Israel
1973	*Yom Kippur* War
1979	Peace treaty between Egypt and Israel
1982	War in Lebanon
1983	Start of mass immigration of Jews from former Soviet Union
1993	Oslo Agreements
1994	Implementation of Palestinian self-government in Gaza Strip and Jericho area. Israel-Jordan Peace Treaty signed
1995	Prime Minister Yitzhak Rabin assassinated at peace rally
2000	Beginning of second Intifada, after Prime minister Barak offered Palestinians the most far-reaching concessions since the signing of the Oslo agreements

AT-A-GLANCE

Jewish Beliefs and Values

Tanach: **The Bible**

The Jewish people is also known as the People of the Book. All our beliefs and values find their origins in our sacred literature. Historical events, scientific insights and sociological developments have led to reinterpretations, re-evaluations and sometimes even to the revival of our beliefs and values. To gain any insight into Jewish belief in all of its variations and to get any understanding of where and why these variations occur, we ought to start with the texts that have carried us through the centuries and have been our source of inspiration and identification.

When counting each book individually, the Bible is composed of 39 books. The Bible is traditionally known by its Hebrew acronym of *"Tanach."* This acronym is a combination of the first letters of the three major sections. The first letter of the Hebrew name of the first section – Torah ("Law") – is combined with the first letters of the two other sections – *Nevi'im* ("Prophets") and *Ketuvim* ("Writings"). Since the *K* of *Ketuvim* can also be read as a gutteral "ch," the combination of letters leads to the word *"Tanach."*

According to Jewish tradition, however, the Bible contains only 24 books: I Samuel and II Samuel are counted as one book; I Kings and II Kings are counted as one book; the 12 Minor Prophets are counted together as one book; the Book of Ezra and the Book of Nehemiah comprise one book; and I Chronicles and II Chronicles comprise one book.

Torah

Since the Torah consists of the Five Books of Moses, it is also known as *Chumash*, which is the Hebrew word for "five" (its Greek equivalent being the Pentateuch: five books). Traditionally, Torah is read on three mornings each week: Monday, Thursday, and Saturday. Each week the portion follows a progressive pattern so that in one year (and according to an ancient Palestinian custom, in three years) the entire Torah scroll is read. Each week's reading is called a *"sidrah"* (from the Hebrew word *seder*, "order") and is ordered by the Hebrew calendar.

To gain any insight into Jewish belief in all of its variations and to get any understanding of where and why these variations occur, we ought to start with the texts that have carried us through the centuries and have been our source of inspiration and identification.

In contrast to the Christian tradition, which has tried to create titles for the five books that reflect the content of the whole book, Judaism follows a less literary approach. It simply takes the first significant word of the first verse of each book as the title.

The contents of the books

a) Beresheet ("In the beginning"), or Genesis. *Beresheet* tells the story from the creation of the world to the death of Joseph in Egypt. The first eleven chapters deal with universal history, and the remainder with the lives of Abraham, Isaac, Jacob, and their families. According to tradition, the total elapsed time adds up to 1946 (or 1948) years. The overriding thrust is the establishment of God's role in human affairs and of man's interaction with God, other human beings, and the self.

b) Shemot ("Names"), or Exodus. *Shemot* is a natural continuation of *Beresheet*. Where *Beresheet* describes the lives of the Patriarchs of the Hebrew people, *Shemot* tells the beginning of the people itself. It records Israel's enslavement in Egypt and the deliverance from the house of bondage. It describes the institution of Passover, the covenant at Mount Sinai, and the organization of public worship that was to make Israel into "a kingdom of priests and a holy nation." It recounts the murmuring and backslidings of Israel, as well as the Divine guidance and instruction vouchsafed to it; the apostasy of the golden calf, as well as the supreme Revelation that followed it — the Revelation of the Divine Being as "God." *Shemot* contains nearly all the foundations on which Jewish life is built, from the Ten Commandments and the historic festivals to the leading principles of civil law

c) Vayikra ("And He called..."), or Leviticus. *Vayikra* contains only a few bits of narrative. It is essentially a compendium of law. In *The Torah: A Modern Commentary* (UAHC) Bernard J. Bamberger numerated this compendium as follows:
- Laws of sacrifice
- The dedication of the Tabernacle and the ordination of the priests, with certain attendant events
- Dietary laws
- Laws of defilement and purification

Beresheet tells the story from the creation of the world to the death of Joseph in Egypt.

Where Beresheet describes the lives of the Patriarchs of the Hebrew people, Shemot tells the beginning of the people itself.

- The Day of Atonement
- Additional laws about sacrifice and food
- Permitted and forbidden sexual relations
- The Law of Holiness – ethical and ritual
- Laws for the priesthood
- The Sabbath and festival calendar
- Two laws and an incident involving blasphemy
- The sabbatical and jubilee years
- An exhortation, containing blessings for the observance of the law and curses for its violation
- Laws concerning vows, gifts, and dues

d) *Bamidbar* ("In the wilderness"), or Numbers. *Bamidbar* starts with extensive statistical material in the opening chapters and has an underlying desert motif. This book continues where *Shemot* left off, as God's special people Israel is subjected to special laws and obligations which are designed to safeguard its holiness. As the narrative unfolds, we are told how Israel continues to fall short of its goals and how God, time and again, is disappointed with His people. Though individuals were punished and a whole generation was condemned to perish in the wilderness, the covenant was not abrogated. The sanctuary, with its Divine manifestation, remained in the midst of the camp, and God never ceased to guide and protect. (To many this period of wandering is seen as a trial of faith.) At the end of *Bamidbar* the vision emerges of a new nation which will go on to possess the Holy Land as a Holy People.

e) *Devarim* ("Words"), or Deuteronomy. The oldest name of this book is *"Mishneh Torah"* ("repetition of the Torah"), a description of its contents found in Chapter 17:18. Although *Devarim* has an affinity with the four previous books in historical, legal, and narrative senses, it is unique in its oratory style. We read how the Lawgiver (God) has brought Israel to the borders of the Holy Land and, through Moses, recounts in three discourses the events of the forty years of wanderings. He warns against the temptations awaiting them in Canaan. He promises Divine judgment for disobedience as well as diving blessing for faithful observance of the *mitzvot* (commandments). As *Devarim* concludes, Moses addresses his people and blesses them for the last time before he dies. Joshua is appointed leader over the

As the narrative unfolds, we are told how Israel continues to fall short of its goals and how God, time and again, is disappointed with His people.

We read how the Lawgiver (God) has brought Israel to the borders of the Holy Land and, through Moses, recounts in three discourses the events of the forty years of wanderings.

people and is ordained by Moses. Moses is buried, "and no one knows his burial place to this day" (34:6). "Never again did there arise in Israel a prophet like Moses – whom the Lord singled out, face to face" (34:10).

Prophets, or *Nevi"im*

Immediately after reading the *sidrah*, a selection from *Nevi'im* is read. There is always some similarity or connection between that which is read from Torah and that which is read from *Nevi'im*. This reading is referred to as "*Haftorah*" ("conclusion"). This tradition stems from the time when Jews were prohibited from reading the Torah by Roman rulers. To keep the ethical messages of the Torah alive, selections of the Prophets reflecting similar messages were found and recited.

The contents of *Nevi'im* are divided into 21 books which are arranged in two parts:

a) The Former Prophets (Nonliterary Prophets). We encounter this group of prophets in the narrative of the story of the settlement of the people in Canaan, the development of God's community. Many of the biblical characters are considered to have the status of "prophets," judges, or leaders (Joshua, Samuel, Elisha, Deborah, David, Elijah, etc.). These characters at the earlier stage of the history of the period of national life did not leave any writings themselves; hence, this section is described with the terms "former" and "nonliterary." The Former Prophets consist of six books: Joshua, Judges, I and II Samuel, and I and II Kings.

b) The Latter Prophets (Literary Prophets). These prophets are situated in the period from the eighth century B.C.E. to the fifth century B.C.E. and each of them has a message for the people of Israel who have strayed collectively from the moral path. They are all considered God's messengers and each has been chosen to speak out about the ills of society. They do not foretell the future in the strict sense of the word, they only tell what could happen if the people do or do not repent. The Latter Prophets are divided into the Major Prophets (those whose books are lengthy): Isaiah, Jeremiah, and Ezekiel; and the Minor Prophets (those whose books are relatively short): Hosea, Joel, Amos, Obadiah, Jonah, Micah, Nahum, Habakkuk, Zephaniah, Haggai, Zechariah, and Malachi.

To keep the ethical messages of the Torah alive, selections of the Prophets reflecting similar messages were found and recited.

These prophets are situated in the period from the eighth century B.C.E. to the fifth century B.C.E. and each of them has a message for the people of Israel who have strayed collectively from the moral path.

Writings, or *Ketuvim*

This is the third and last section of the *Tanach* and totals thirteen books. It is a mixed anthology of literary pieces and stories relevant to the Jewish people. Although in existence before, these writings were officially admitted to the Bible (canonized) by 90 C.E.

Its contents:

a) Poetic Books:

1. Psalms: The doubts, hopes, desires, prayers, and faith of the authors.
2. Proverbs: Cogent sayings pertaining to living.
3. Job: The story of how Satan, with God's consent, tested Job to learn if Job was really as righteous as he appeared.

b) The Five Scrolls, each of which is read in the synagogue in scroll form on one of the Jewish holidays:

1. Book of Esther: *Purim.*
2. Ecclesiastes (deals with the purpose and the often futile nature of life): *Sukkot.*
3. Song of Songs: *Pesach.*
4. Story of Ruth: *Shavuot.*
5. Book of Lamentations: *Tishah B'Av.*

c) Prophetic Books:

1. Daniel: Stirring faith in God.

d) Historical Books:

1. Ezra
2. Nehemiah
3. I Chronicles
4. II Chronicles

The Origin and Growth of Jewish Law

Torah

The Torah is the first and main source for the laws of the Jewish religion. The most important laws and teachings of Jewish faith, such as the belief in one God, the Ten Commandments, the observance of the Sabbath and the majority of Jewish festivals, the Jewish Dietary Laws, the duties to wear *tefilin* and fringes, the *mezuzah*, the laws of morality and justice, are all found in the Torah. Traditional Jews believe that these laws are not the inventions of any man's mind but were revealed by God to Moses. Our ancestors accepted the teachings of Torah for all times and regarded it as the holiest constitution of our people, which is binding on every generation. Today, traditional Jews still accept the laws of the Bible as the direct work of God, and therefore consider them to be sacred, eternal and applicable to all times and conditions. Other branches of Judaism have other views on the origins of the Torah. The chapter on Revelation will give you a more comprehensive treatment of this issue.

Today, traditional Jews still accept the laws of the Bible as the direct work of God, and therefore consider them to be sacred, eternal and applicable to all times and conditions.

Mishnah

Jewish law did not stop growing after the completion of the Bible. The laws of the Torah were not sufficient to serve as a guide for daily conduct. Some biblical laws were either too brief or not explicit enough, not containing the details as to how they were to be observed. Furthermore, in the course of the centuries, the conditions of Jewish life changed and some laws had to be revised or adjusted to be applicable to new circumstances. It also became necessary to add new ordinances to enable our people to carry out some of the biblical laws.

The religious teachers and rabbis of each generation after the Bible felt the need to clarify and expand the biblical laws and add many detailed regulations as to how they were to be observed. These additional laws

Jewish law did not stop growing after the completion of the Bible.

were taught orally and were handed down from one generation to another. This constantly expanding body of new laws became so voluminous that it was no longer possible to preserve it as oral tradition. It had to be edited, classified in systematic form and written down. This post-biblical collection of laws is called the "*Mishnah*," or the "Oral Law."

In the first century, Rabbi Hillel began to arrange the laws of the "*Tanaim*," the rabbis whose legal opinions form the *Mishnah*. His work was continued by Rabbis Akiva, Ishmael, and Meir and was completed in the year 200 C.E by Rabbi Judah of Palestine, whose scholarly stature and ethical personality were so revered that he became known as "The Prince." He classified the laws of *Mishnah* and wrote them down in Hebrew.

The *Mishnah* is divided into six main divisions, termed "orders" or "*sedarim*." Each order, in turn, is divided into a number of tractates or "*Masechtot*." The tractates are divided into chapters.

The six orders are:

1) Zeraim ("Seeds"): The laws relating to the cultivation of the soil and the produce thereof.

2) Moed ("Festivals"): The laws concerning the observance of the Sabbath and holidays.

3) Nashim ("Women"): The laws concerning marriage, divorce, and problems connected with family.

4) Nezikin ("Damages"): This order contains most of the civil and criminal laws, including the intricate details of court procedure.

5) Kodoshim ("Holy Things"): Laws pertaining to sacrifices and Temple Services.

6) Taharot ("Purities"): The laws of purity and impurity.

Gemara

As time passed, the laws of the *Mishnah* themselves became incomplete and inadequate to meet the needs of changing circumstances in Jewish life. It didn't take long for the *Mishnah* to become the object of explanation, debate and addition. New situations had to be addressed. There were differences in opinion as to the exact meaning of laws in the *Mishnah*. There was a kaleidoscope of interpretations of rabbis who lived after the

As time passed, the laws of the Mishnah themselves became incomplete and inadequate to meet the needs of changing circumstances in Jewish life.

Tanaim. All these opinions and discussions were collected and written down and served as a commentary to the *Mishnah*. This commentary came to be known as the *"Gemara"* ("completion"). The rabbis whose opinions are found in the *"Gemara"* are known as *"Amoraim."*

The *Gemara* was recorded about the year 500 C.E. The *Mishnah* and *Gemara* were edited together in a collection called the Talmud, which means "teaching." The work of developing the *Gemara* was carried out simultaneously in the rabbinical academies of Palestine and Babylon – so that we have two versions of the Talmud: the Palestinian Talmud and the Babylonian Talmud. Of these two versions the Babylonian Talmud is widely regarded as the more complete and more authoritative. Next to the Bible, the Talmud is the highest and most important source for the Jewish law. The Talmud has had a tremendous influence on Jewish life throughout the centuries. It was the guide by which for almost 2000 years our fathers regulated the conduct of their daily lives and affairs, as well as their religious customs and ceremonies.

Next to the Bible, the Talmud is the highest and most important source for the Jewish law. The Talmud has had a tremendous influence on Jewish life throughout the centuries.

What We Find in the Talmud

The Talmud contains a complete code of Jewish law. However, it is much more than just a collection of laws. Instead of a mere legal code, it contains discussions about the different laws and it branches out into discussions of various subjects. We find in these discussions such subjects as science, history, legends, ethics, and moral teaching. Yet the most important part of the Talmud remains its legal opinions. The legal parts of the Talmud are called *"Halacha,"* and the non-legal parts are called *"Aggadah."* These parts are not separated in the text of the Talmud, but intermingled.

Codes

Although the primary sources for all our religious laws are the Bible and the Talmud, the task of finding a legal decision in the vast collection of Talmudic books was difficult and at times confusing.

The Bible itself is ambiguous and therefore needed commentary, which we find in the Talmud. However, the rabbis in the Talmud did not always reach a final fixed ruling. And to make things more complicated, the laws in the Talmud are not arranged in a logical, systematic order. Some laws are discussed in different sections. Since the Talmud is a large collection of books, similar to a vast encyclopedia, it would require an individual to have great skill and scholarship, and to devote lots of time in order to locate a legal ruling in the Talmud.

This situation made it necessary to write a code, a collection of all Talmudic laws, arranged logically and systematically according to subject matter. A code does not include complicated discussions or reasons for the laws — it merely gives the final decisions.

Throughout history great minds have attempted to develop the perfect code that would change chaos into order and would derive easy insight from complex matters. Some of these codes faded into oblivion, while others became so authoritative that they are still in use today. Those that have made it to the present day are:

1. The *Mishneh Torah*, or "The second Torah," written in the 12th century by Moses Maimonides. His famous code, known as *"Mishneh Torah"* ("The second Torah") or *"Yad Hachazakah"* ("The strong hand"), contains all the laws of the Talmud arranged systematically in a total of fourteen books. It was a huge undertaking and is a legacy of the genius of Maimonides. The *Mishneh Torah* is considered not only to be a brilliant exercise of codification, but also the greatest work in rabbinical literature.

2. The *Arba Turim*, or "The four rows." Jewish law continued to grow, and new material accumulated in the rabbinical school of France and Germany after the finalization of Maimonides' work. A new code was necessary. Rabbi Jacob ben Asher of the 14th century wrote a new code known as the *"Arba Turim"*, which was a standard practical code of law in its day.

3. The *Shulchan Aruch*, or "The Prepared Table." This code, which serves as the basis for Jewish practice in the Orthodox Jewish world even today, was compiled by Rabbi Joseph Karo in the 16th century. It became the most popular and authoritative code for all Jews. It contains a complete collection of all laws governing all actions in Jewish life. The code includes laws of prayer, Sabbath, festivals, *Kashrut*, property, marriage, divorce, mourning, charity, business regulations, honesty and how one is to feel with his fellow men. The *Shulchan Aruch* differs from the preceding codes because it was in-

Throughout history great minds have attempted to develop the perfect code that would change chaos into order and would derive easy insight from complex matters.

The **Shulchan Aruch** *differs from the preceding codes because it was intended for the use of laymen.*

tended for the use of laymen. It is a handy manual, a simple and concise law book which can be understood by the lay person. (An abridged English version by Ganzfried and Goldin is available.)

4. *A Guide to Jewish Religious Practice*, by Isaac Klein. This volume is a detailed and comprehensive guide to Jewish practice for the home and synagogue, written in the spirit of the Conservative movement. The many subjects treated in this volume are discussed in the light of traditional Jewish sources (Bible, Talmud, Law Codes, Responsa literature, etc.). The topics covered include virtually everything that might be of interest to the modern Jew: the laws of *kashrut* and how to keep a kosher home; the meaning and significance of the holidays and how to observe them at home and in the synagogue; laws governing such key life events as marriage, divorce, birth, adoption, conversion, death, and many others. The volume also includes full discussions, from the Jewish point of view, of such pressing issues of current concern as euthanasia, organ transplantation, abortion, autopsy, artificial insemination, and women's rights.

Basic Beliefs

The Thirteen Principles of Maimonides

One cannot assert that there are dogmatic "articles of faith" in Judaism, as one would when referring to Christianity or Islam. Throughout history there have been several attempts to systematize the basic beliefs of Judaism. However, the acceptance of these formulations has always depended on the authority of the rabbi or scholar who created them. Doubtlessly, the most famous is the formulation created by Maimonides (13th century): the "Thirteen Principles of Faith." With time, these principles have acquired a quasi-dogmatic character, although *Halacha* does not establish the obligation to believe in them. The summary of these principles is as follows:

I believe with complete faith that:

1. God exists.
2. God is one.
3. God is incorporeal.
4. God is the beginning and eternity.
5. God alone is to be worshipped.
6. prophecy occurs.
7. the prophecy of Moses is true and superior to that of all other prophets.
8. the Torah we have was revealed to Moses on Mount Sinai.
9. this Torah will never be altered.
10. God knows all human acts.
11. God rewards the righteous and punishes the wicked.
12. the Messiah will come.
13. the dead will be resurrected.

Other Approaches

In the Middle Ages, the successors of Maimonides, such as Nachmanides, Abba Mari ben Moshe, Simon ben Zemah, Duran, Isaac Arama,

One cannot assert that there are dogmatic "articles of faith" in Judaism, as one would when referring to Christianity or Islam.

and Joseph Chaabez, reduced these thirteen principles to only three: belief in God, Creation (or Revelation), and Providence/Retribution. Others, such as Crescas and David ben Samuel Estrella, spoke of seven fundamental principles. David ben Yom-Tov ibn Bilia, in his *Yesodot HaMaskil*, adds another thirteen of his own principles to those of Maimonides. And Yedaiah Penini, in the last chapter of his *Behinat HaDat*, lists 35 basic principles of the Jewish faith.

In the 14th century, Asher ben Chehiel of Toledo opposed the principles formulated by Maimonides, declaring that they were only temporal and that one more should be added to expressly recognize that the Exile was a punishment for the sins of Israel. Isaac Abravanel, in his *Rosh Emunah*, defended the principles of Maimonides but refused to accept dogmatic principles for Judaism from the point of view (shared by the Kabbalists) that the 613 *mitzvot* were equivalent to any formulation.

The Principles of Faith and Contemporary Judaism

While no formulation or creed has been fully accepted by all Jewish currents throughout history, there are certain elements which enjoy an unarguable consensus and which will be studied, albeit briefly, in the following chapters: the existence of one God, the nature of Revelation, and the ideas relating to the world to come.

Isaac Abravanel, in his **Rosh Emunah,** *defended the* **principles of Maimonides but refused to accept dogmatic principles for Judaism.**

God in Judaism

The Existence and Nature of God

Before we begin and as we will explore later on, one has to know that Judaism does not impose a dogmatic belief in a given idea of God. Different Jewish thinkers, from different times, have envisioned God in many different ways. For some, "He" is not an external being. For others, the vision is a pantheistic one... In this text, when speaking of God, the pronoun used will be "He." Nevertheless, this does not presuppose that God is an external being or exclusively masculine. We use this pronoun solely due to considerations of linguistic economy.

The idea of one God is, perhaps, the greatest contribution of the Jewish people to humanity. The *Sh'ma* prayer, the prayer that a devout Jew recites twice daily and is, when circumstances make it possible, his last utterance before dying, is indeed a declaration of this belief in God's uniqueness: "Hear, oh Israel, the Lord is God, the Lord is One" ("*Sh'ma Israel, Adonai Eloheinu, Adonai Echad*").

Despite the fact that the belief in one God, who is incorporeal and immaterial, is undisputed, there have been different ways of understanding this Divine presence throughout history. Centuries ago, the compilers of the *Siddur* ("prayer book") expressed the impossibility of a single, uniform experience of God when the *Avot* prayer was created. This prayer, expressing the merit of our ancestors, begins with: "Blessed are You, Oh Lord our God. God of Abraham, God of Isaac, and God of Jacob." The repetition of the phrase "God of" instead of the more compact formulation, "God of Abraham, Isaac, and Jacob" is not accidental. The author of this prayer was expressing something very clearly: Although each one of the patriarchs believed in the same God, each one experienced that God differently.

The individual experience of the Divine does not mean that any concept of God is compatible with Judaism. For instance, the belief that a human being can be God, or part of a God, is not acceptable for Judaism.

Despite the fact that the belief in one God, who is incorporeal and immaterial, is undisputed, there have been different ways of understanding this Divine presence throughout history. Although each one of the patriarchs believed in the same God, each one experienced that God differently.

Since Judaism considers the human being as something finite, one cannot be considered (or worshipped as) something Divine.

Although we can give only a brief overview, it is interesting to touch upon some of these historical Jewish concepts of God which allow every Jew to find his or her own place within the Jewish tradition.

God in the *Tanach*

Neither in the Torah nor in the rest of the Hebrew Bible is there any passage that proves the existence of God. That God exists is the central premise that is a given in the Bible. The *Tanach* is not a description of *what* God is like, but rather of His relationship with the people of Israel. The idea of that God which can be deduced from the biblical text, is characterized by the following aspects and attributes:

1. Monotheism. There is only one God. As opposed to other gods in Antiquity, God does not have a counterpart of the opposite sex, or any mythology (or history: parents, children, siblings). God is strictly one, as is asserted throughout the Bible.

2. God has a Name. In the Bible, there are several expressions used to refer to God. *El* or *Elohim* (God), *El, Shaddai* (Almighty), *Adon* (Lord), *Tzur* (Rock), *Av* (Father), or *Melech* (King) are a few of them. But in the Bible, God also has a proper name, consisting of the four Hebrew consonants *Yud Hay Vav Hay*, which has no clear meaning and is most likely to come from a Hebrew verb meaning "existence." In reality, we do not know how this tetragram is pronounced. In the past, there were no vowels used in Hebrew and the Bible provides no hints as to how the name is correctly pronounced. Let's use an example. Imagine the Hebrew name *DBR*. Depending on which vowels we use and how they are arranged, it could, for instance, be pronounced as "Dibra" or "Dobro." Only if we know the vowels can we pronounce it correctly: "Deborah." Although the Israelites of biblical times surely knew the Name, its use was so restricted that it wasn't common knowledge, like everything else in the Bible was. Out of the fear of misusing God's name, a group of scribes from the sixth and seventh centuries (known as the Masorites) decided that the most appropriate reading for the name of God should be *Adonai* ("my Lord"), although this pronunciation bears no resemblance to

Neither in the Torah nor in the rest of the Hebrew Bible is there any passage that proves the existence of God. The *Tanach* is not a description of *what* God is like, but rather of His relationship with the people of Israel.

any of the consonants (*YHVH*). Since the name of God was so scarcely used and later on replaced by a synonym, the knowledge of the proper vowels to add to the consonants eventually got lost altogether. Even today, many Jews do not write the word "God" completely, but rather use such expressions as "G-d." This practice is directly related to biblical times. Tellingly, one of the names of God is *HaShem*, or "The Name."

3. Nobody knows God's appearance. In the Bible there are many references to God's "hands" and "eyes." But it has always been considered that these words were simply literary techniques to make an otherwise totally abstract concept more or less tangible. God has no form. We can feel His presence, but not know what He looks like.

4. God acts in the world. We cannot describe God in human terms, but we can recognize His presence in the beauty of nature, which He created, and in His influence in human history.

5. God has a special relationship with Israel. In the Talmud we read that Jews were "chosen" only after other peoples rejected the Torah and its obligations. Being chosen does not imply a privilege, but rather a great responsibility, as many prophetic writings state. The meaning of this notion has been, and continues to be, one of the most misunderstood elements of Judaism.

6. Israel has a Covenant with God. And this Covenant is eternal, as the Bible reminds us repeatedly each time Israel transgresses. It does not only affect the Israelites who were present at Mt. Sinai, but all future Jewish generations, including us. As has been pointed out earlier, in a *Midrash* it is asserted that the souls of all Jews of all time were present on the day the Covenant was made. (This, of course, gave way to conflicts regarding our interpretation of the Covenant. Judaism does not separate body and soul, which is a major difference from Christianity. Therefore, if our bodies were not present, some say, "legally" we were not present and the Covenant can be considered null and void.) This Covenant, which constitutes the founding of Judaism, transforming the Israelites into a people by faith and no longer a people by fate, imposes duties and obligations to both parties: God and the Israelites. God commits himself to protect Israel and Israel must be faithful to Him and follow the conditions of the Covenant. Yet the God of the Bible is also a compassionate God. And a

Being chosen does not imply a privilege, but rather a great responsibility, as many prophetic writings state. The meaning of this notion has been, and continues to be, one of the most misunderstood elements of Judaism.

Judaism does not separate body and soul, which is a major difference from Christianity.

day will come, as the prophet Jeremiah states, when external laws will no longer be necessary to obey the Covenant; rather, all the laws will be in the hearts of all men and women; it will be their second nature.

7. *God expects ethical behavior of man.* The biblical God of Israel is a source of ethical values. The rituals and fulfillment of the laws are not enough. More than anything else, God expects man to behave with goodness, rectitude, and above all, justice. Judaism is defined as a way of *being*, of acting in this world, not as a series of beliefs.

8. *God is a personal God.* God is compassionate and merciful, and He listens to man. Although this is a generally accepted concept of God, throughout history several important Jewish thinkers, most notably Albert Einstein, have rejected this notion of a personal God.

9. *We cannot understand why the righteous suffer in the world.* One of the topics that appear constantly in the Bible is that of rewarding the righteous and punishing the wicked, despite the fact that at times the opposite is true. There is no one answer in the Bible, and Jewish thinkers throughout history have interpreted this in many different, sometimes contradictory, ways, especially after the Holocaust.

What cannot be said about God in this book

In the 1st century one of the most important thinkers of all times was born, Philo Judeus (popularly known as Philo of Alexandria). His fundamental ideas about God are the same as those of the Talmudic rabbis who were exploring the attributes and aspects of God that can be deduced from biblical texts as we have seen in the previous section. Philo made an outstanding effort to harmonize Greek and Jewish culture, which led to certain divergences or different interpretations of the Divine. Philo believed that the only way to define God is through His negative attributes, that is, what God is *not*. This way, the expression "God is just" is inadequate because we cannot have a specific idea of what that justice really is. To say, on the other hand, that God is not unjust is a surer way of approaching His reality.

Philo's different approach to describing God is only one of many attempts to give insight in the Divine. Thousands of years of history, the absence of central dogma, and the constant efforts of great thinkers to ap-

Judaism is defined as a way of being, of acting in this world, not as a series of beliefs. God is compassionate and merciful, and He listens to man. Although this is a generally accepted concept of God, throughout history several important Jewish thinkers, most notably Albert Einstein, have rejected this notion of a personal God.

ply new philosophical insights to Jewish theology make it impossible to give a complete overview in this context.

Between the early explorations of Philo, the approach to God through the Neo-Aristotelianism of Maimonides and the mysticism of Luria in medieval times, the influence of Descartes on Spinoza in later centuries, and the thoughts of more contemporary minds like Buber with his dialogical philosophy, the limited theism of Steinberg, the humanism of Kaplan, the fusion of psychoanalysis, humanism and Marxism by Fromm and the existentialism of Emmanuel Levinas, there is a myriad of insights into and explanations of the nature of the Divine. All are Jewish ways of thinking and feeling *shechinah*, the Divine presence. And they are all equally valid and equally Jewish.

The concept of God in Judaism has never been static. By contrasting the biblical idea, which still dominates Christianity as a dogma, with the general postures of the different Jewish movements, one will realize how varied Jewish thought really is. No movement forwards an idea of God as a creed, but they do try to offer an idea open enough to give a coherent explanation of how the Jews of each movement conceive their relationship with God, with religion.

The concept of God in Judaism has never been static.

For instance, Reform Jews accept the principle of Maimonides that affirms that God exists and that God is one, but they add that there is no agreement, and nor should there be, because it is a personal matter of each Jew, on how to understand or envision that God. Reconstructionists affirm: "God is the source of meaning. We struggle with doubts and insecurities. We affirm that struggle; we believe that it is the duty of all Jews to question and study to find his or her own personal path to the Divine. We believe in a God that inhabits this world and especially the human heart. God is the source of our generosity, sensitivity, and preoccupation for the world that surrounds us. God is also the power within us that pushes us towards self-realization and ethical behavior. We find God when we look for the meaning of the world, when we feel the motivation to study, and when we work towards morality and social justice."

Reform Jews accept the principle of Maimonides that affirms that God exists and that God is one, but they add that there is no agreement, and nor should there be, because it is a personal matter of each Jew, on how to understand or envision that God.

Instead of trying to summarize this ocean of interpretation and approach, this book would rather help you to develop an appreciation for all these different thoughts.

Revelation

Orthodox Judaism believes that the Revelation of Torah was supernatural: Moses ascended Sinai in the midst of thunder and lightning to hear, literally, the words of the Ten Commandments and of the Torah, spoken by a Divine voice. Non-Orthodox interpretations vary from God steering man in his understanding of the Divine to Revelation as being man's own understanding of the Divine.

How is the Eternal revealed to humankind? This fundamental question has sparked very different answers and attitudes in Judaism. It is so basic that the answer to this question is what separates Orthodox from non-Orthodox movements. Orthodox Judaism believes that the Revelation of Torah was supernatural: Moses ascended Sinai in the midst of thunder and lightning to hear, literally, the words of the Ten Commandments and of the Torah, spoken by a Divine voice. Non-Orthodox interpretations vary from God steering man in his understanding of the Divine to Revelation as being man's own understanding of the Divine.

There have always been Jewish leaders, even many years ago, who have considered the biblical passages and descriptions relating to Revelation as poetic representations of the natural order, not the supernatural one. Today, a significant number of rabbis would say that wherever and whenever a human being reaches new goals in creation or in his or her appreciation of the truth, then and there Revelation has occurred. The scientist in his or her laboratory, the composer at the keyboard, the artist in front of his or her canvas: they all can experience Divine Revelation when they are open to experiencing it as such and are willing to communicate with the Divine.

Our own way of communicating with God is through prayer. As is customary in Judaism, we can expect to find very different opinions among Jewish thinkers on this subject. Some believe, as did the majority of our ancestors, that each word that we utter is a prayer heard by a Divine ear. Some may even believe that it is possible, through prayer, to change Divine intention, although very rarely in Jewish history has this position been adopted. Others consider that prayer is any variety of reading, thought, or meditation that reinforces our relationship with the Eternal, that reminds us of our valuable heritage and our ultimate purpose, which stimulates us to break the barrier between what we are and what we can become, and to try to achieve the latter. Jewish religious naturalists would define prayer as any intellectual, emotional, or esthetic experience that reinforces our spiritual relationship with the universe. For them, prayer is analogous to reminding one's self of one's ultimate goal in the journey of life, why it is important to reach that goal, what the best methods and routes are, what resources are available to guarantee that one will reach that goal safely. The Jewish religious naturalist does not expect prayer to change God's will or God Himself; instead, it activates the God in each of us and makes possible the kind of behavior and the degree of spiritual realization that otherwise would be impossible.

There is enough room within Judaism for supernaturalist and naturalist interpretations of Revelation and prayer. The similarities between these interpretations are more important than the differences. In both cases, the Jew trusts that, in the universe and his or her own life, there exists a spiritual essence with which it is possible to establish a dialogue and through which his or her personal journey can be enriched and elevated.

Orthodox Judaism considers the *mitzvot* and *Halacha* to be obligatory, the supreme measure of the Jewish quality of a life. This is because Orthodoxy believes that God revealed Himself to Moses on Mt. Sinai and that this Revelation included absolutely everything, both in content as well as in time. The answer to any question that a student could possibly ask today, has already been revealed at Mt. Sinai. One will find the answer (God's will) through the study of the text and by following *Halacha*.

Generally speaking, liberal Judaism believes that Revelation is ongoing. God is a radio station that is constantly broadcasting, but only a few people turn on their receptor and listen to what is being said. All scientific discoveries are forms of Revelation, and we adapt our understanding of the Jewish Law to the times, precisely because Revelation is not static. The Torah was not given to Moses by God, but was rather the result of many generations of inspired thinkers, and it reflects how our ancestors thought about God, how the Eternal revealed Himself to other generations that, just like us, lived in a specific place at a specific time. As Buber or Heschel would say, the *mitzvot* and *Halacha* do not contain Revelation, but are rather a specifically Jewish way of how the human soul responds to the Eternal, an objectified dialogue, a human answer to Revelation, an attempt to describe the Divine presence in a human way.

Orthodoxy believes that God revealed Himself to Moses on Mt. Sinai and that this Revelation included absolutely everything, both in content as well as in time. Generally speaking, liberal Judaism believes that Revelation is ongoing.

*The opinions
on, for instance,
homosexuality,
illustrate the division
in understanding the
nature of Revelation.*

The opinions on, for instance, homosexuality, illustrate the division in understanding the nature of Revelation. The Orthodox follow the literal meaning of the famous passage in Leviticus that prohibits homosexuality. Non-Orthodox Judaism interprets this passage in many different ways, including the idea that this prohibition is only a cultural reflection of the time Leviticus was written. In fact, the non-Orthodox rabbinical organizations in the U.S. were pioneers in the struggle for the full rights of gays and lesbians. They were the first institutions not only to accept gays and lesbians, but also to motivate their congregants to educate other Jews on the need to participate in the struggle for equal rights. Judaism, in this sense, has been very faithful to its tradition of constant evolution. Generally speaking, Judaism has also gained the adhesion of gay and lesbian Jews, instead of provoking conflict and alienation.

Olam HaBa:
Ideas on the World to Come

The term "world to come," or "*Olam HaBa*," has a double meaning in Judaism. On one hand, it refers to the afterlife, the space that exists after death. On the other hand, the same term is used to refer to this world after the coming of the Messiah. Both concepts are complementary and at times are confused; due to this, it is convenient to study them separately.

Death and the World to Come

Judaism firmly sustains that death is not the end of human existence. Maimonides includes the belief in the resurrection of the dead as one of his thirteen basic principles of the Jewish faith. But at the same time, we should highlight that in Judaism there exists no formal eschatology, but rather a kind of traditional consensus regarding ideas and beliefs. There is no clear idea of Paradise, Hell, and Purgatory, as there is in Christianity or Islam.

But before explaining how these beliefs in death and the afterlife, which in reality are not explicitly explained in the Torah, entered the Jewish belief system, it is necessary to remember that Judaism is a religion which focuses fundamentally and emphatically on life (*chai*). In the Talmud, we can read that on Judgement Day we will be judged not only based on our sins, but on those pleasures which we had at our disposal but we refused. Asceticism and privations are, since the beginning of Judaism, simply and flatly sins (inasmuch as they are an attack on the natural course of life), and during the time of the Temple, the ascete had to offer a sacrifice in order to pay for his voluntary privations. Maimonides himself wrote, "If, for instance, a non-Jew threatens to kill a Jew unless he or she transgresses any precept mentioned in the Torah, the Jew must transgress it and not be killed, for it is written: 'The man who fulfills them will live for them.' He will live for them, and not die for them. He who allows himself to be killed in order to avoid transgressing is guiltier than if he were transgressing."

There is no clear idea of Paradise, Hell, and Purgatory, as there is in Christianity or Islam. In the Talmud, we can read that on Judgement Day we will be judged not only based on our sins, but on those pleasures which we had at our disposal but we refused.

Next to this emphasis on life, there is the pragmatic attitude that it is better to put your thought and energy into matters you can find answers to, like whether one can use an egg that was laid by a chicken on Shabbat, instead of wasting time by speculating on matters that will never have a clear answer: the afterlife. In the **Tanach** *there is only one brief mention of the world to come.*

Next to this emphasis on life, there is the pragmatic attitude that it is better to put your thought and energy into matters you can find answers to, like whether one can use an egg that was laid by a chicken on Shabbat, instead of wasting time by speculating on matters that will never have a clear answer: the afterlife. Therefore, at the very heart of Orthodox Judaism one can find completely different concepts on the afterlife living side by side: a heaven similar to that of the Christians where the souls of the righteous, the souls which are awaiting the coming of the Messiah, go after death, and the belief in reincarnation and the transmigration of souls (*gilgulim*), which has been profusely detailed by the Kabbalists.

Biblical and Talmudic References

In the *Tanach* there is only one brief mention of the world to come. In Exodus 15:1, while the Hebrews cross the Red Sea, it says that "Moses and the children of Israel sang" or "Then Moses and the children of Israel will sing (in the future)." This is the only "proof" found in the Bible, for if Moses is dead and the Torah says that he will again sing, it is a sign that somehow he will return to life. Besides this, the Bible contains no direct references either to Heaven or to Hell as a place where human beings go after death. Chapters 2 and 3 of Genesis (*Beresheet*) and chapter 28 of the book of Ezekiel mention a worldly Garden of Eden (*Gan Eden*), but it does not allude to the heavenly paradise mentioned in later Jewish works. The concepts of Heaven and Hell were not a matter of serious debate among Jews until after the destruction of the first Temple in 586 B.C.E. and the subsequent expulsion of the Jews from Babylon.

During Talmudic times, especially during the Roman persecutions of the first centuries of the Common Era, the concept of Heaven and Hell took root among the Jews. Heaven was compared to *Gan Eden,* or Paradise. The translation of the Bible into Greek calls *Gan Eden* a "Paradise," a word which probably comes from Persian and simply means "park" or "garden." The Garden of Eden was thought of as a place where the righteous would enjoy the results of their virtuous lives on Earth after their deaths. Simultaneously, the idea was spread that those who were not righteous on Earth, would be condemned to Hell (*Gehinom*). The Hebrew word "*Gehi-*

nom" is the same as the Greek word *"Gehenna."* The book of Joshua (15:8) and Kings II (23:10) describe *Gehinom* as the "valley of the son of Hinom," a place located south of Jerusalem where children were sacrificed to the God Molok. This valley became known as a cursed place and the word *"Gehena"* became a symbol of all that is evil and sinful.

Many rabbis of the Talmudic period viewed Paradise and Hell as places really created by God. The Talmud says that the famous Rabbi J. ben Zakkai wept before his death because he was not sure whether he would go to Heaven or Hell. And there are likewise many Talmudic sources that speak of Paradise and Hell as physical spaces.

As is the case with every subject, it is not easy to find conclusive and dogmatic answers in the 15,000 pages of the Talmud on matters of Heaven and Hell. Nor did the discussion come to an end after the Talmud was completed. Therefore, for the erudite rabbi of the 3rd century, Aba Aricha (known as Rev), Paradise is a spiritual place. Maimonides was of the same opinion: "In the world to come there are no bodies or corporeal forms, only the souls of the righteous..." And one hundred years later, in the 13th century, Rabbi Moshe ben Nachman (Nachmanides) said that *Gen Eden* is a "world of souls" *(Olam HaNefashot)*.

As for the "resurrection of the dead," there is a famous reference in the vision of the prophet Ezekiel and in the book of Daniel (12:2-3): "Many of those that sleep in the dust of the Earth will awake, some to eternal life, others to reproaches, to everlasting abhorrence. And the knowledgeable will be radiant like the bright expanse of sky, and those who lead the many to righteousness will be like the stars forever and ever." The Talmudic rabbis affirm that the Jew who does not believe in the resurrection of the dead excludes himself or herself from the Jewish people and will not have a place in the world to come.

All major Jewish movements agree on the immortality of the soul. But there are substantial differences. The traditional or Orthodox *Siddur* (prayer book) includes very specific allusions to Paradise, Hell, and the physical resurrection of the dead. In one of its central prayers, the *Amidah* includes constant references to resurrection: "You sustain with mercy the living, you reawake the dead (...) Oh King who orders to die, to resurrect, and to

As is the case with every subject, it is not easy to find conclusive and dogmatic answers in the 15,000 pages of the Talmud on matters of Heaven and Hell.

Generally speaking, the Orthodox still believe in resurrection, which will occur when the Messiah comes, as well as in the immortality of the soul. Reform Jews tend not to believe in resurrection, but they do believe in a spiritual life after death. Their emphasis is placed on the memory of the dead and in our way of living in this world.

be saved (...) Faithful are You to resurrect the dead. Blessed be You, oh Lord, who resurrects the dead." But in Reform *Siddurim*, which also contain the *Amidah*, these references have been changed for others such as "...who saves" or "...who makes wonders." In the prayer books of the Conservative movement, many of these allusions are maintained so that the one who is praying can interpret them as he or she sees fit. Generally speaking, the Orthodox still believe in resurrection, which will occur when the Messiah comes, as well as in the immortality of the soul. Reform Jews tend not to believe in resurrection, but they do believe in a spiritual life after death. Their emphasis is placed on the memory of the dead and in our way of living in this world. Conservative Jews have maintained the idea of resurrection and of the immortality of the soul in their liturgy. Many believe in these ideas in a figurative or poetic sense, not a literal one.

The Messiah and *Olam HaBa*

The coming of the *Mashiach*, or the Jewish Messiah, will inaugurate a time in which all the righteous in the world (both Jews and non-Jews) will participate in a perfect world, *Olam HaBa*. The righteous of the past will be resurrected in order to be able to participate in that world which they helped to create, while the evil simply will not be waken and they will not be able to participate.

In the *Mishnah*, there are many opinions regarding that world to come of the Messiah. It says, for instance, that this is a world like the day before the Sabbath (*Erev Shabbat*) and the world to come is like the Sabbath itself. The Talmud includes commentaries on how the observance of the *mitzvot* guarantees a larger or smaller participation in the world to come. These allusions have always been considered hyperboles and literary registers. We must remember, once again, that Judaism is not a religion that focuses on the world to come, it is not about how to enter Heaven, but rather how to live on Earth. For traditional Judaism, fulfilling the 613 *mitzvot* has nothing to do with reaping a reward in the world to come. It is a privilege and an obligation for Jews, and they should expect nothing in return. One of the ethical books of the *Mishnah*, *Pirkei Avot*, which still has tremendous relevance today, clearly says that one must not act like a wage earner who works solely in order to earn a salary and a reward.

As for the figure of the Messiah and his coming, there are many and very different interpretations which have appeared over the course of Jewish history. One can read, for instance, that the *Mashiach* will arrive on the day that all Jews observe the Sabbath halachically. This example, as well as many others, clearly expresses that the Jewish people has always understood that we must actively work on this Earth in order to prepare it for the coming of the Messiah. It is not enough to remain seated, passively praying and waiting. Rather, one must promote here and now the values of justice which are typical of Judaism. One must *act* to make this world a better place, and a more just place (*tikkun olam*, or "reparation of the world"). Reform Jews, especially, emphasize this idea, which they term "ethical monotheism." For them, ethics is more important than ritual.

Because Reform Judaism takes a different approach, it also has a different view of the idea of a Messiah and the world to come. Orthodox sources see the *Mashiach* as a human of flesh and blood that will arrive on a specific date. Liberal movements concentrate on working at the realization of a Messianic Era, promoting justice day by day in order to create a world without pain.

Non-Jews (Gentiles) and the World to Come

During the time of the writing of the Talmud there were some opinions contrary to the participation of Gentiles in the world to come, as they were seen as evil. But the majority of opinions, from the Talmud to Maimonides, establish that the righteous of each and every nation will have a part in the world to come.

This issue is related to the often misinterpreted idea of "Chosen People." The Talmud says that God offered the Torah to many nations, but only the last one, the Jews, accepted. The Talmud makes it clear that *Adonai* is the God of both Jews and Gentiles. However, for Jews there are more responsibilities than there are for Gentiles precisely because they were chosen. For traditional Judaism, Jews must fulfill 613 *mitzvot* in their daily lives in order to be saved, while Gentiles need only fulfill 7, the famous Noahide Laws:

One must act to make this world a better place, and a more just place (tikkun olam, or "reparation of the world"). Orthodox sources see the Mashiach as a human of flesh and blood that will arrive on a specific date. Liberal movements concentrate on working at the realization of a Messianic Era, promoting justice day by day in order to create a world without pain.

1. Do not murder.
2. Do not steal.
3. Do not worship false gods.
4. Do not practice sexual immorality.
5. Do not eat the limb of an animal before it is killed.
6. Do not curse God.
7. Set up courts and bring offenders to justice.

This brings us to one of the historical justifications of the lack of proselytism in Judaism and the traditionally passive attitude towards conversions. In colloquial terms what is being said is: If you are going to have a place in the world to come because you are righteous anyway, why become Jewish? And on top of that: Since Jews have more responsibilities, it's so much harder to be regarded as righteous, so why do you want to make life difficult by becoming a Jew?

Differences among Jewish Movements

In the preceding chapters, some of the differences among contemporary Jewish movements have been reviewed. A monolithic belief system does not exist in Judaism, and you can find many differences within the various movement themselves. As has been pointed out, it is more appropriate to speak of "approaches to Judaism" than of different forms of Judaism, as this usually leads to a discussion on who or what is more Jewish. One is not "more Jewish" simply because one follows tradition. Each movement reflects a living form of Judaism that is present throughout the world. Each of these approaches represents a different path to the same God.

This chart only attempts to highlight the differences of opinion regarding some key issues in Judaism today.

	Orthodox	Conservative	Reform	Reconstructionist
God	Personal deity whose providence is a reality	Several different interpretations, ranging from supernaturalism to naturalist humanism	Several different interpretations, with a wide range for different opinions for naturalists, supernaturalists, and religious humanists	The power which makes human salvation possible; the source of the highest human values and transcendental feelings
Torah	Of Divine origin, given to Moses on Mt. Sinai	The word of God, revealed but not literal, given to us through human transmission	Written by hand by humans, with Divine inspiration; other points of view are accepted	The effort to achieve salvation, self-realization; a collection of writings done by a series of people; belief in Divine inspiration but not in Revelation

AT-A-GLANCE

	Orthodox	Conservative	Reform	Reconstructionist
Halacha	Eternal, irrevocable, must be followed; it is the Orthodox guide and only the rabbinic sages can reinterpret it and adapt it to new situations	In favor of preserving tradition, but consider that it can change in the fact of modern needs; rabbinical decisions are accepted	The ethical aspects are the Revelation of God and are accepted; the ritual *mitzvot* are a way of promoting spirituality; individuals have autonomy to decide if they accept *Halacha*	Considered a custom; commitment to tradition and search for contemporary meaning; communities adapt *Halacha* to their own democratic procedures; rabbis are teachers who work with the lay members to establish norms
Women	Different roles and duties; seated apart in the synagogue; only men can become rabbis and cantors; a *minyan* is not relevant to female prayer and women are not counted towards a *minyan*	They assume the same role as men in the majority of rituals and practices; they can be part of a *minyan*, sit with men in the synagogue, and become rabbis and cantors	Total equality in all rituals and practices; they can be part of a *minyan*, sit with men in the synagogue, and become rabbis and cantors; there is a symbolic *brit milah* ceremony for women	Total equality in religious life and liturgy; women sit with men, can be part of a *minyan*, and become rabbis and cantors
Kashrut	Obligatory to follow the laws, according to Orthodox interpretation of them	Obligatory to follow the laws, according to Conservative interpretation of them	Jews are encouraged to study the laws and follow those which increase the sanctity of their life and their personal relationship with God	Considered a custom; encouraged as a way of enriching one's commitment and Jewish identity
Brit milah	Obligatory	Obligatory	Obligatory for all born Jewish males	Obligatory
Divorce	Document required *(get)*	Document required *(get)*	*Get* not required	An egalitarian *get* is exchanged by the husband and wife
Interfaith Marriage	Prohibited	Prohibited	Normally opposed; there are some rabbis who will officiate; mixed couples are welcomed at synagogues	Rabbis participate if the couple participates in the community; some only require that the couple keep a Jewish home and raise their children as Jews; are welcomed at synagogues

AT-A-GLANCE

Time in Judaism

The Life Cycle

Our lives are defined by two of the most mysterious moments we can comprehend: birth and death. Between beginning and end there are numerous moments in our life that mark transition or transformation. Entering into adulthood, the start of one's own family, becoming a parent, loosing a loved one… Judaism recognizes the significance of these moments that mark one's life and has developed rituals that allow us to experience these moments to their fullest extent. It's the Jewish way of living life.

The destruction of the Temple in Jerusalem (586 B.C.E.) gave birth to the Diaspora: a culture without a homeland. Jewish life became decentralized, and the home and the synagogue became the cohesive pillars of the Jewish community. They perpetuated Jewish culture through the observance of Jewish practices related to the life cycle. The home, seen as a sanctuary, and the family are the cornerstones of Jewish life. Each Jewish ritual has an aspect that takes place at home, with the family, and an aspect that takes place in the synagogue, with the community. Some holidays are celebrated exclusively in the home and others, such as *Yom Kippur*, are centered around the synagogue.

The home, seen as a sanctuary, and the family are the cornerstones of Jewish life.

Birth

If Judaism is known for one thing, it is how it values its children, who are considered the most precious gift, a blessing. There are many explanations for this attitude, from religious motives found in the *Tanach* to more practical reasons, such as the need to perpetuate a small and scattered Jewish population. The relationship between children and parents is strongly emphasized and the obligations of each party to the other are highly valued, as is the importance of education. One important thing to remember is that Judaism does not know any concept of original sin. A Jewish baby is born without sin or guilt of any kind. Without an innate burden or heritage of any kind, a Jewish child holds a promise for the future.

One important thing to remember is that Judaism does not know any concept of original sin.

There are many customs surrounding the birth of a baby. Many families plant a tree, usually in Israel, to mark the birth of a child. This custom stems from an old Talmudic tradition of planting trees at the birth of children. When the boy and girl grew up and got married, branches of their trees were used for their *Chuppah,* the wedding canopy.

A Jewish child gets two names, one for secular use and one for religious use, such as when one is called to the Torah.

A Jewish child gets two names, one for secular use and one for religious use, such as when one is called to the Torah. In Ashkenazi tradition, the child's secular name is often that of a deceased relative, as a homage to that person, expressing the hope that the deceased's qualities will live on in the newborn. According to Sefardi tradition, the baby is named after a living relative. Usually, the secular name is still a biblical name, thereby creating a rather long list of "typical Jewish" names. Some of the most common secular names are Aaron, Jacob, Michael, David, Rachel, Sarah, Beth and Judith.

When a Jewish boy is born, he must be circumcised on the eighth day after birth, according to God's command to Abraham in the book of Genesis.

When a Jewish boy is born, he must be circumcised on the eighth day after birth, according to God's command to Abraham in the book of Genesis. This ceremony is called *"brit milah."* The commandment that circumcision must take place on the eighth day is so overriding that the ceremony is performed even if it falls on Shabbat or on *Yom Kippur. Brit milah* is a mark of Jewish loyalty and a sign that one is a son of the Jewish faith. Immediately after the circumcision the child is given a name as part of the ceremony. Because no time proscription is given in the case of a girl, she receives her name in the synagogue on a Shabbat shortly after birth, when the father is called up to the Torah. Reform tradition emphasizing the equality of the genders encourages that a baby naming for a girl, a *Brit Bat,* also takes place on the eight day after birth.

The tradition known as *Pidyon Haben* dates from the time of the Temple. When the first born child in a family is a son, the father must redeem his son from the priest (*kohen*) on the thirty-first day after the birth. The origin of this tradition is that the first-born male child belongs to God and has to be redeemed through the *kohen* who represents God. A ceremony is conducted, the father recites a prayer and hands the *kohen* five shekels, which the *kohen* usually donates to charity. If the father or mother comes from a *kohen* or levite family, the redeeming of the first born does not take place. This tradition is not followed by non-Orthodox Jews, who do not recognize the hierarchical division between Israelites and *Kohanim* and *Levim,* or the supremacy of the first born.

Education

The emphasis Judaism puts on education is not just for the sake of intellectual exercise, but to fulfill one of the Biblical commandments which states that one ought to teach the words of God diligently to one's children.

In the tradition of the Old World, a Jewish boy would start his education at the age of three by learning the Hebrew alphabet. A drop of honey was put on each letter as an incentive to master the letter, to instill the sweetness of Torah in the little boy. Today it's customary to celebrate the beginning of a child's religious education with the ceremony of Consecration. Normally this takes place during the holiday of *Simchat Torah*, thus aligning the start of a new cycle of Torah reading with the beginning of a child's Jewish education.

In modern times, the ceremony of Confirmation was instituted both for girls and boys by the non-Orthodox denominations of Judaism. At the age of sixteen, boys and girls who have attended a religious school are qualified to enter into an everlasting and solemn treaty with God and Israel. They pledge themselves to the observance and sanctification of the laws, teachings, and traditions of Judaism. The Confirmation services are held on the first days of *Shavuot*, an agricultural holiday by origin that has been transformed into a celebration of the giving of the Torah at Mt. Sinai. By affirming a future life connected to Torah, the confirmants resemble those who were present at that most defining moment in Jewish history.

Bar Mitzvah

When a boy reaches the age of thirteen, he becomes a full-fledged member of the Jewish community and is known as a *Bar Mitzvah* ("a son of duty, or of the commandment"). At this age he becomes responsible for his actions and is obligated to obey the religious laws, customs and observances of our faith. Traditionally he is also required to don *tefilin* at the appropriate times, at morning services except for Shabbat and holidays. In 14th-century Rhineland, the ceremony was developed for a boy to be called up to read from the Torah in the synagogue for the very first time in his life

The emphasis Judaism puts on education is not just for the sake of intellectual exercise, but to fulfill one of the Biblical commandments which states that one ought to teach the words of God diligently to one's children.

on the Sabbath succeeding his thirteenth birthday. It's customary for the boy to chant the *Haftorah*, but at times he also reads part of the weekly portion of the Torah. This occasion is usually marked by a party and festive celebration given by the parents in his honor.

Bat Mitzvah

For some years, it has been practice in Reform, Conservative, and Reconstructionist synagogues to enable girls to become *Bat Mitzvah* at the age of twelve. To qualify for the *Bat Mitzvah* ceremony, girls have to prepare in the same ways as boys, attending Hebrew school classes three or more years prior to their *Bat Mitzvah*.

The idea of a Bat Mitzvah was developed by Mordechai Kaplan, the founder of Reconstructionist Judaism.

The idea of a *Bat Mitzvah* was developed by Mordechai Kaplan, the founder of Reconstructionist Judaism. It was his daughter Judith who became the first girl to ever have a *Bat Mitzvah* ceremony in 1922. Where some congregations limit the ceremony by letting her participate in the Friday night services only, in other synagogues the *Bat Mitzvah* girl chants the *Haftorah* at the Shabbat morning service.

Marriage

Judaism regards marriage as a religious act and as a holy union. The Hebrew word for a wedding is *kidushin*, sanctification. To make the marriage valid Jewish law requires that both parties enter the marriage on their own free will and that both parties are Jewish (the issue of interfaith marriages is discussed later in this chapter).

The wedding ceremony is celebrated under a canopy, known as a chuppah, which is made up of four poles with a covering of silk or satin, usually richly embroidered.

The wedding ceremony is celebrated under a canopy, known as a *chuppah*, which is made up of four poles with a covering of silk or satin, usually richly embroidered. The *chuppah* symbolizes the future home of the couple. First the groom is led to the canopy, usually to the accompaniment of music, and then the bride is brought in. The officiating rabbi recites seven blessings over a cup of wine from which the groom and bride drink. The groom then places a ring on the second finger of the bride's right hand and pronounces the following words: "Behold you are consecrated unto me with this ring according to the Law of Moses and of Israel." This part of the ceremony is the most important element of the marriage. Jewish law requires that this statement be made in the presence of two witnesses. The ring should be a plain gold band and traditionally does not contain jewels because, without any additions, the round shape of the ring expresses more clearly the unity without beginning or end, the eternal relationship between bride and groom.

It is customary for the rabbi to deliver a brief talk and to bestow his or her blessings upon the couple. The ceremony is concluded with the breaking of a glass by the bridegroom. This is an ancient custom to remind us of the destruction of the Temple and of our ancient homeland at joyous occasions. It also shows us that marriage is less solid than we like to think, and that we need to make a mutual and constant effort to keep it from "breaking." After this, the assembled guests offer good wishes (*Mazal Tov!*) to the married couple.

The *ketubah*, the Hebrew marriage contract, is often a beautifully illustrated and illuminated art work that legalizes the marital bond of the couple. The importance of the religious aspect of the marriage in a Jewish household is often reflected by displaying the *ketubah* as a cherished family heirloom.

Although not traditionally Jewish, many Jewish couples today like to celebrate their silver or golden anniversary by renewing their wedding vows, either by a Jewish ceremony that reflects the original wedding or by one of the contemporary ceremonies.

The ceremony is concluded with the breaking of a glass by the bridegroom. This is an ancient custom to remind us of the destruction of the Temple and of our ancient homeland at joyous occasions. It also shows us that marriage is less solid than we like to think, and that we need to make a mutual and constant effort to keep it from "breaking."

The Question of Interfaith Marriages

One of the results of the open American society of today has been a rise in the rate of marriage between Jews and Gentiles. While the rate is still much lower than in, for example, the Catholic community, it is alarming from the point of view of the continuity of Jewish tradition. Previous experience has indicated (and sociological studies have affirmed) that about 70% of the children of a interfaith marriage are not raised as Jews. Thus, widespread interfaith marriages could threaten the survival of the Jewish people. However, where the Gentile becomes Jewish we do not have an interfaith marriage; we have a Jewish marriage. The number of such "New Jewish" marriages seems to be rising at an even faster rate than the number of interfaith marriages. Thus, the answer for the Jewish community is not to withdraw from the open society but rather to encourage Gentiles who fall in love with Jews to extend their involvement to the religious sense as well; and for Jews to welcome them into the household of Israel.

Religious reasons are not the only ones that make a people hesitate about interfaith marriages. Marriage counselors and sociologists indicate that the divorce rate in interfaith marriage is twice as high as that of marriages within the same faith. Also, the children of interfaith marriages are often troubled as to their identity, and the statistics show that such children have a higher rate of difficulty with the police. For these and religious reasons Conservative and Orthodox rabbis and the majority of Reform rabbis will not perform marriages when one of the partners is not Jewish. Those rabbis who do perform interfaith marriages each have their own motivation to do so.

Marriage counselors and sociologists indicate that the divorce rate in interfaith marriage is twice as high as that of marriages within the same faith.

God Loves Love:
Why I Officiate and Co-Officiate at Interfaith Marriages*

Some say God is love. Even after years of rabbinical study I still can't give such a clear-cut definition of the Divine Being, but I do know God loves love. Love is God's major gift to us. We are blessed when we are so much in love that we wish to spend the rest of our lives together.

As a rabbi I feel blessed when I am invited by a couple to share in the confirmation of their love, whether both partners are Jewish or not. Generally, when a Jew and Gentile fall in love, they have a hard time finding a rabbi willing to participate in their wedding. While there can be many good reasons for a rabbi not to officiate at interfaith weddings (which is not for me to dispute), to me such a position doesn't encourage future choices in favor of Judaism by the couple. In my nine years as a rabbi no couple has ever asked my point of view on interfaith marriage – rather they ask for my help. My choice, therefore, lies in whether or not I help them at this pivotal moment in their lives.

In my nine years as a rabbi no couple has ever asked my point of view on interfaith marriage – rather they ask for my help.

I have come to realize that the non-Jewish partner (and his or her family) is as entitled to having a member of the clergy they feel comfortable with as is the Jewish partner. So, I will co-officiate at a service that, while

---

* This article originally appeared on InterfaithFamily.com and is reprinted with permission. Visit www.InterfaithFamily.com to find over 600 articles of interest to people with interfaith relationships and those who work with them.

true to both traditions, does not have elements that could be perceived as offensive by either party. What is sacrificed in religious "integrity" by crafting a non-denominational service is little compared with the harmony that is created at this defining moment of the couple's life.

Rather than talk about issues that divide the couple, such as belief in Jesus, the other officiant and I talk about God and love. At the same time, elements and rituals from both traditions are a wonderful addition to any wedding, so we may use the traditional Jewish seven blessings, breaking of the glass, and *chuppah* (wedding canopy), the Christian Unity candle, biblical readings, exchange of vows and rings, etc. When selecting readings from the Bible, I ask the couple to use texts from the New Testament that are appropriate and neutral, such as Paul's letter to the Corinthians, which talks about love, rather than sections that refer to Jesus. A very nice touch I like to add is doing the priestly benediction at the end of the ceremony jointly with the other officiant. We recite it line by line, I in Hebrew and the other officiant in English. That is a very nice sign of unity at the end of the ceremony.

Although the ceremony itself is non-denominational when I co-officiate, I do stress a very important Jewish concept known as *shalom bayit*, "peace in the home." The Jewish emphasis on family life is a topic on which I tend to counsel couples in great detail, and we discuss their life together and specially issues of raising children in an interfaith family. I don't believe that interfaith couples have more problems than others, it's just that their problems have extra dimensions. I like to remind all couples that the key to marital success is communication. I believe certain issues are better discussed ahead of time, such as children and religious practices in the home. Clearly, as a rabbi I would prefer that the couple decided to raise their children Jewish. However, that does not mean I wouldn't officiate at a wedding for a couple that is still trying to decide what to do. I am a strong believer that children should be raised with one clearly defined religion, but that does not prevent the parents from exposing their child to the other religion, maybe at the home of the other set of grandparents.

I will co-officiate with any clergy who are is as open minded as I am, always focusing on the couple's wants and needs. I believe that, as clergy, we must be there to support the couple and to show them that religion

Rather than talk about issues that divide the couple, such as belief in Jesus, the other officiant and I talk about God and love.

Although the ceremony itself is non-denominational when I co-officiate, I do stress a very important Jewish concept known as shalom bayit, "peace in the home."

can have a place in their joint lives, even if they come from different faiths. Couples and their families tend to be very happy with the ceremonies I participate in, mainly because I attempt to make the wedding a reflection of who the couple is and what they want their ceremony to be and convey. I make sure that each wedding is unique, as no two couples are alike. I respect each couple's right to make a choice that works for them, and if they choose to claim a place in the Jewish community, I am delighted to welcome them at the moment they officially establish their future together.

Serving my congregation, The New Reform Temple in Kansas City, is my primary obligation, but I am very grateful to them for being understanding and allowing me to officiate at weddings for non-members in town. When my agenda allows, I also officiate at weddings in other parts of the Midwest, throughout the United States and even abroad. The fact that people are willing to fly a rabbi from far away is to me a testimony of the great value they place on Judaism and the great efforts they are willing to go through in order to have a Jewish element in their lives. How could I not respond positively to such an affirmation of Yiddishkeit (love of Judaism)?

Commitment ceremonies

As modern Judaism is constantly seeking answers to contemporary developments, the issue of same-sex commitment ceremonies has become very important. Although it has to be stated very clearly that today's laws do not give any legal authority to same-sex unions, clergy of any faith has to respond to a growing number of requests to perform such ceremonies and to add a spiritual meaning and blessing to the commitment two people have for each other.

For each individual member of the clergy, taking a position on this issue is finding a balance between faith, dogma, and personal responsibility. Some rabbis will perform commitment ceremonies providing both partners are Jewish, whereas a minority of rabbis will perform interfaith same-sex commitment ceremonies.

Divorce

Judaism recognized the concept of "guiltless" divorce thousands of years ago. It has always accepted divorce as a fact that can occur in life, albeit a

As modern Judaism is constantly seeking answers to contemporary developments, the issue of same-sex commitment ceremonies has become very important. Some rabbis will perform commitment ceremonies providing both partners are Jewish, whereas a minority of rabbis will perform interfaith same-sex commitment ceremonies.

sad one. Judaism acknowledges that it is better for a couple to be divorced than to remain in a state of constant anger and bitterness.

This does not imply that Judaism takes divorce lightly. Many aspects of Jewish law do not approve of it, and the procedural details related to divorce are complex and demanding. Except in certain cases of a wife's misconduct, the husband must pay her a considerable amount, according to the stipulations in the *ketubah* ("wedding contract"). Furthermore, Jewish law prohibits a man from remarrying his ex-wife if she has married another man. The *Kohanim* (priests) cannot marry divorced women.

According to the Torah, divorce procedures entail writing a declaration of divorce, delivering it to the wife, and sending her out of the house. In order to impede men from getting an unwise divorce, the rabbis created complex rules to be followed in the writing of the document, in its delivery, and in its acceptance. A competent rabbinical authority must be consulted for any divorce. The document is called a *Sefer K'ritut* in the Talmud, although today it is usually called a *get*. There is no negative terminology; the traditional text does not recreate the negative aspects of the marriage, nor does it specify the reason for the divorce. Instead, it states that the woman is now free to marry another man. It is not necessary that the husband deliver the *get* personally. If it is not possible or desired that the couple meet, a messenger can deliver it. It is important to remember that a civil divorce is not sufficient to dissolve a Jewish marriage. As for Jewish law, the couple remains married until the wife receives the *get*.

Reform Judaism does not require a *get*, recognizing a civil divorce as sufficient to terminate a Jewish marriage.

Sickness

Although sickness cannot be planned like a wedding, a *bar* or *bar mitzvah* or even birth for that matter, it is part of life. As it is a Jew's obligation to follow the many examples of God's goodness reflected in the Torah, so is visiting the sick (*bikkur cholim*) considered a *mitzvah*, a religious obligation. In the book of Genesis we read how God visited Abraham as he was recovering from his circumcision, so is it our responsibility to visit the sick. According to the rabbis it is counted among "the fruits of which

In order to impede men from getting an unwise divorce, the rabbis created complex rules to be followed in the writing of the document, in its delivery, and in its acceptance.

Reform Judaism does not require a get, recognizing a civil divorce as sufficient to terminate a Jewish marriage.

a person enjoys in this world, but the stock remains even in the hereafter." However, the rabbis also warn us to show restraint in fulfilling the *mitzvah* of *bikkur cholim*. We ought to be mindful that we don't make visits at an inappropriate time, or that our visit lasts too long.

It is also part of life that sickness can lead to death. In this day and age, where medical technology confronts us with ethical dilemmas and even forces us to make decisions of life and death, it is worth mentioning that Judaism confronted the essence of euthanasia centuries ago in the Talmud. The basic premise is that a dying person is considered the same as a living person in every respect. And since we have to choose life, active euthanasia is considered murder. However, the same ethical principles tell us that it is as much a sin to prolong suffering. To quote the Talmud: "If there is something that causes a delay in the exit of the soul, as for example, if near his house there is a sound of pounding like one who is chopping wood, or there is salt on his tongue, and these delay the soul's leaving the body, it is permitted to remove these, because there is no direct act involved here; only the removal of an obstacle. (...) One may not cause the slowing of the dying process. For example, if one was dying and another person near that house was chopping wood and because of this the soul was not able to depart, they remove the wood chopper there. (...) One should not cry out upon him (today we would say, apply artificial stimulants), that his soul should return since he cannot live thereby but a short time and those days he will suffer pain."

Once the final moment is there, how is death determined in Jewish tradition? Traditionally a person was pronounced dead when he or she stopped breathing and his or her pulse stopped. As late as 1971, the Chief Rabbinate of Israel declared "brain death," which is generally accepted as the new criterion for determining death, to be inadmissible. Later technology, especially in the measurement of brain activity, has convinced authorities to change that position. They suggested the following criteria for defining death: a flat EEG reading (in the absence of any signs of life), the severance of any vital organs, and the fracture of the body into two parts.

As for transplants, there is no greater *K'vod Hamet* (respect for the dead) than to bring healing to the living. Therefore, some accept this practice,

The basic premise is that a dying person is considered the same as a living person in every respect. And since we have to choose life, active euthanasia is considered murder. However, the same ethical principles tell us that it is as much a sin to prolong suffering.

which is nevertheless rejected by more traditional individuals. With regard to cremation, the Jewish way of burial is to place the body into the earth, as suggested in the biblical verse, "and to dust thou shall return." Due to this, and to the fact that it violates the integrity of the body, cremation is frowned upon, but nonetheless accepted by the majority of Reform rabbis. If it is necessary (required by civil law or if there must be a delay in burying), embalming is allowed. But only the type of embalming where the body remains intact is permitted.

Death, Mourning, and Afterlife

Jewish mourning practices have evolved to respond to the psychological needs of the person who has lost a loved one. In this sense, they are not mere ritual formalities but instruments to help the living. Their aim is to accompany the mourner through all the psychological phases and guide him or her once again towards a full life. After all, Judaism is a religion that affirms life should be lived to its fullest.

The purpose of Jewish laws and customs dealing with the burial and mourning is to offer comfort to the relatives of a deceased person during the time of sorrow and bereavement. These laws of mourning aim at assuring the bereaved family that God, the author of life and death, is a merciful and loving father. They express the comforting thought that, though we may not understand why our dear departed were taken from us, they are at peace under God's protective care.

When it appears that the moment of death is near, the dying patient is expected to confess his or her sins and ask for God's forgiveness. If he or she is no longer able to speak, others recite the confessional prayer (*Vidui*) for him or her. This prayer concludes with the declaration of faith, "Hear, O Israel, the Lord our God, the Lord is One." Also, "Praised be His name whose glorious kingdom is forever." When death finally comes, those present say, "Blessed art Thou the True Judge." By this statement the Jew acknowledges that, though death is tragic, it must be accepted with courage. Soon, the immediate relatives perform the *Keriah* custom by making a slight tear in their outer garment as a symbol of grief, or in a small piece of cloth called a *Keriah* ribbon. Present practice requires tearing the garment only for

Jewish mourning practices have evolved to respond to the psychological needs of the person who has lost a loved one.

the relatives for whom one has to observe the mourning period: mother, father, son, daughter, brother, sister, husband, or wife. In *Keriah* for one's father or mother, the garment is torn on the left side, where the heart is.

The body of the deceased is bathed and cleaned in preparation for burial. This purification (*taharah*) is done by the *Chavurah Kaddishah* (the burial society, literally the "Holy Society"). The law requires that the dead be dressed in shrouds (*tachrichim*) of white linen or cotton to emphasize the equality of all in death. In Jewish tradition, viewing the deceased, as is custom in Christian burial rites, is not considered to be respectful to the dead. A person's last right should be the right of utter privacy, the privilege of remaining untampered with after death.

It is regarded a *mitzvah* (a religious duty) for the relatives and friends of the deceased to participate in the funeral procession. A special service is held at the burial ground. Similar to the use of shrouds it is customary to use simple wooden coffins. This shows that in the final moment we are all equal, it saves the poor from embarrassment and moreover, it avoids glorifying death.

Upon returning from the cemetery the first seven days of strict mourning known as *Shivah* begin. One is required to observe *Shivah* for parents, sons and daughters, brothers, sisters, husband, and wife. A memorial light is kept burning in the house of mourning during this week. This practice is based on the biblical saying: "The soul of man is the lamp of God." Regular services are held in the house of mourning, both in the morning and the afternoon, so that the mourners may recite the *Kaddish* during the week.

The mourners are seated on low stools, without shoes, as a sign of humility. This is the most central of the observances that accentuate the grief of the bereaved during this period. Another observance is the covering of mirrors in the home. The mirror is a symbol of human vanity which is out of place in a house of mourning. Likewise, bathing and anointing are forbidden if for pleasure; they are permitted for hygienic or medical reasons. Shaving and cutting the hair are also forbidden. Women should not use cosmetics.

The mourners abstain from their ordinary occupations and stay home during the seven days of *Shivah*. There is no *Shivah* on Shabbat or on major

In Jewish tradition, viewing the deceased, as is custom in Christian burial rites, is not considered to be respectful to the dead. A person's last right should be the right of utter privacy, the privilege of remaining untampered with after death.

holidays, and mourners attend services in the synagogue. The exemption from mourning on Shabbat does not apply to things done in private.

Throughout this period, relatives and friends visit the mourners to console them. It is common to bring food already prepared to the home of the mourner (it is typical to bring hard-boiled eggs and lentils, which symbolize fertility and life). Visitors should avoid speaking of trivial matters and should listen to the mourners, so that the mourners can set the tone of the conversation. There are moments when one can only express sadness and grief, there are moments our psyche yearns for fond memories. As visitors, we help the mourners expel the strong emotions that one feels after the loss of a loved one. Similarly, friends should avoid giving gratuitous psychological advice.

The first month after death is known as *Sh'loshim*, the thirty days of mourning (which includes the seven days of *Shivah*). During this period, the mourners return to work, but abstain from attending festive occasions; they are not to visit places of amusement and they are to avoid listening to music. The *Keriah* ribbon is worn during the whole of this period, except on the Sabbath. When losing a parent the period of mourning continues for a whole year.

Children mourning for departed parents are required to recite the *Kaddish* at the daily morning and evening service for eleven months. This period was originally twelve months, but was reduced because twelve months was regarded as the maximum period of punishment for the wicked in the heavenly court and, should the mourner say *Kaddish* for twelve months, it would suggest that the child considered his or her parents as deserving the maximum penalty. If a person dies childless, the nearest relatives may say the *Kaddish* for him. *Kaddish* is also recited on every recurring anniversary of the death of a parent, known by the Yiddish name of *Yahrzeit*.

The *Kaddish* prayer contains nothing pertaining to death. It is a hymn of praise to God. It is a prayer for the coming of the day when God's kingdom will be established on Earth, when all mankind will worship the one God and when universal peace will be established. The purpose of *Kaddish* is to give the mourner the opportunity to express his or her faith in God and in His justice and to submit to His will even at the time of sorrow.

*The **Kaddish** prayer contains nothing pertaining to death. It is a hymn of praise to God. It is a prayer for the coming of the day when God's kingdom will be established on Earth, when all mankind will worship the one God and when universal peace will be established.*

Beyond one's own interpretation, what is truly affirmed in the Kaddish *is hope in a moment of pain, solidity in a moment of weakness. Life. It helps us return to life and rebuild our inner strength.*

Judaism does not have a clearly defined concept of an afterlife as can be found in other religions.

As with other areas of Jewish practice, the way one understands the prayer varies with each person. One can recite *Kaddish* with the notion that every person contains the image of God and that, since part of God's image has left with the death of a loved one, God is asked to fill this void by magnifying himself. *Kaddish* can be recited out of gratitude, thanking God for giving us the ability to love. The physical presence of a person may be taken away from us, but the love we have for the deceased is everlasting. Beyond one's own interpretation, what is truly affirmed in the *Kaddish* is hope in a moment of pain, solidity in a moment of weakness. Life. It helps us return to life and rebuild our inner strength.

Perhaps the highest purpose of the Mourner's *Kaddish* is that, by reciting this ancient prayer, the mourner affirms his or her belief in God and his or her loyalty to Judaism and publicly declares his or her intention to carry on the religion of his or her parents. It means that the religion of the deceased parent will live on in the hearts of his or her children.

Judaism does not have a clearly defined concept of an afterlife as can be found in other religions. Although some of the prophets paint visions of what could be in the hereafter and throughout the ages Jewish thinkers have addressed an array of possibilities of the afterlife, the general notion is that we can better focus on what we can know than on what we ultimately will never know.

If there is a generally accepted position on life after death, it is the belief that someone's acts and deeds have influence even after death. When looking for examples to illuminate this position, we tend to think of larger than life figures, philanthropists like Guggenheim, for example, or righteous heroes like Oscar Schindler. Yet every one of us leaves a legacy. A grandfather whose encouraging words gives a child the confidence to have a successful career. A true friend who doesn't shy away from telling you the truth. Even the smile of a stranger on a subway breaking through a sense of loneliness. It is because of this notion of death defying influence of one's acts that Judaism puts great emphasis on remembrance (or, as someone once put it: "We Jews suffer from many ailments, but amnesia is not one of them"). By remembering the dead, we give them an afterlife.

Remembrance is formalized in one's individual obligation to say *Kaddish*. And as every aspect of Jewish life knows both an individual and a community component, there is a special memorial service several times a year by the name of *Yizkor*, which literally means "to remember." It is held during the synagogue services on *Yom Kippur* and on the last days of *Pesach*, *Shavuot* and on the eighth day of *Sukkot*. Each worshipper recites the *Yizkor* prayer silently, mentioning the names of his or her loved ones who have passed away, while the cantor recites a special prayer for the souls of the dead, known as the *"El Maleh Rachamim."*

If you wish to express your sympathy to the bereaved family in a tangible way according to Jewish tradition, make a donation to the deceased's favorite charity, or to the synagogue where he or she worshipped.

The concept of *tzeddakah*, which literally means "justice," plays a central role in Judaism. Although *tzeddakah* unfortunately tends to be translated as "charity," being confused with the Christian concept and its connotations, it is an obligation, since it is an obligation to repair our broken world (*tikkun olam*). *Tzeddakah*, in Judaism, replaces the custom of sending flowers, a common practice in other cultures.

The *Matzeivah* (Setting of the stone) is the dedication of the memorial marker on the grave. This tradition dates back to biblical times, as it says in the book of Genesis: "Jacob set up a pillar on Rachel's grave." The unveiling of the monument usually takes place between one and eleven months after the funeral. The ceremony usually reflects the living legacy of the deceased more than being an opportunity for a second funeral.

The yearly anniversary of the passing of a loved one is commonly known by its Yiddish name, *"Yarzeit."* It is customary for the closest relatives to commemorate the anniversary by lighting a memorial candle at home, making donations to charity in memory of the deceased, and attending services to recite the *Kaddish*.

Although tzeddakah *unfortunately tends to be translated as "charity," being confused with the Christian concept and its connotations, it is an obligation, since it is an obligation to repair our broken world* (tikkun olam).

The Yearly Cycle

The Jewish Calendar

The Jewish calendar is based on the lunar cycle and has adaptations to keep up with the changes of the season caused by the position of the sun.

The Jewish calendar is based on the lunar cycle and has adaptations to keep up with the changes of the season caused by the position of the sun. The time it takes the moon to circle around the earth constitutes a month. The day following the evening on which the moon was first noticed is called *Rosh Chodesh* ("New Moon"). In ancient times this was considered by the Jews as important a festival as Shabbat. Today, while not considered a holiday, special prayers are added to the services and no mourning is permitted on *Rosh Chodesh.* Although not generally practiced, *Rosh Chodesh* has seen a revival since the mid-1970s in pace with the struggle for women's rights as a holiday with a strong feminine component, celebrated by women.

The circling of the moon around the earth takes 29 days, 12 hours and 44 minutes. In order to use round figures and to have each month begin at sunset, it became necessary to add a half day to one month and to take off a half day from the next. The months, therefore, have alternating 29 and 30 days, with the exception of two consecutive months: *Cheshvan* and *Kislev,* which have 29 days each. If the month has 29 days, *Rosh Chodesh* is observed for only one day; when the month has 30 days, then two days of *Rosh Chodesh* are celebrated: the last day of the outgoing month and the first day of the new moon.

An ordinary year consists of twelve lunar months. The names of the months are: *Tishri, Cheshvan, Kislev, Teves, Shevat, Adar, Nisan, Iyar, Sivan, Tamuz, Av,* and *Elul.*

The Jewish year totals 354 days. In itself that would cause no problem in keeping time, if it wasn't for the Bible where it is distinctly ordered that Passover is to be celebrated in the spring, and *Sukkot* to be observed after the harvest in the fall season. To comply with these biblical commandments, it was devised that in the course of 29 years there be seven leap years. During the cycle of 19 years, the third, sixth, eight, eleventh, fourteenth, seventeenth, and nineteenth year have an extra month. The extra month is called *Adar Sheni* (second *Adar*) and is added between *Adar* and *Nisan*.

This is where the Jewish calendar is distinctively different that other calendars. The Muslim calendar, for instance, is also based on the lunar cycle, but since the Koran doesn't have specific stipulations on the seasons when holidays should be celebrated, we see the holy month, or Ramadan, move up 10 days through the seasons every year. The Gentile calendar is based on the solar cycle and consists of 365 days, representing the time of one revolution of the earth around the sun. Because of the difference of 11 days with the lunar cycle and the leap years to keep the Jewish holidays in their designated seasons, it seems as if the Jewish holidays "jump around" in comparison with the Gentile calendar, in a sequence that repeats itself every nineteen years. Remarks like "The High Holidays are late this year" or "*Pesach* is early this year" are basically incorrect, since according to the Jewish calendar the holidays are always on the same date.

In olden times, the start of a new month was announced by the High Court of Jerusalem. Since means of communication were primitive and slow, it often happened that not all the communities could be reached in time. As a result, the Jews who lived far from Jerusalem or even outside of Palestine, were left in doubt as to the correct day of the month. Moreover, it was nearly impossible for them to determine the correct days of the holidays.

To make sure that the exact day was not missed, the High Court in Jerusalem issued the order that Jews outside of Israel should celebrate their holidays one more day in addition to the days commanded in the Bible. That is why an extra day was added to *Sukkot*, Passover (*Pesach*) and *Shavuot*. This practice remained even after the permanent calendar was established by Hillel the Elder, the grandson of the famous Rabbi Hillel, in the year 360 C.E. and the determination of the right dates didn't depend on the High Court anymore. In Israel, however, all holidays, with the exception of *Rosh HaShanah*, have always been celebrated for one day.

As there is no uncertainty as to when the holidays are supposed to be celebrated, Reform Judaism follows the custom of the land of Israel and celebrates the holidays for one day only.

In olden times, the start of a new month was announced by the High Court of Jerusalem.

Shabbat

Anyone who is only slightly familiar with the cycle of Jewish holidays, knows that every week has a Shabbat and that the other holidays, like *Yom Kippur* and *Pesach,* occur only once a year. It would therefore be easy to conclude that Shabbat is the most common holiday and the other holidays are more special. Since that which is more common usually has less value, the more special holidays must have more value.

It might come as a surprise that exactly the opposite is true. The Bible states that those who don't observe *Yom Kippur* will be removed from their kin, while those who neglect Shabbat will be put to death. A clearer statement on which is more holy is hardly possible: Shabbat is without question the most important holiday.

Although in modern thought we might be weary that too much of a good thing might cause it to lose its shine, we should thank God that he has given us such an abundance of His holiest of time.

What Shabbat Means to Us

Shabbat is one of the greatest and most cherished contributions the Jewish religion has made to mankind. The ceremonies of Shabbat serve to strengthen the bonds of love between the members of the family and to deepen the respect of children toward parents.

Shabbat is one of the greatest and most cherished contributions the Jewish religion has made to mankind. The Jews were the first to set aside one day of the week to rest from all labor and be released from the daily burdens, a day of devotion to life's higher purposes that refresh the spirit and delight the heart.

The ceremonies of Shabbat serve to strengthen the bonds of love between the members of the family and to deepen the respect of children toward parents. They also cultivate a deeper appreciation of the laws and teachings of our religion. Through observing Shabbat one not only lives the laws and teachings, one also creates time to study the laws and teachings.

Our ancestors came to regard Shabbat the most cherished gift from God. Shabbat stood out as a pillar of light and strength to our people in all ages and all lands of its dispersion. Amidst persecution, slavery and brutality, Shabbat symbolized that a Jew can be physically subjugated, but that religiously, emotionally, and spiritually he will always be a free man. As one of the great Jewish thinkers of our day, Ahad HaAm, said, "Much more than the Jews preserved Shabbat, Shabbat preserved the Jewish people."

Reasons for Shabbat

The Torah offers two reasons for the observance of Shabbat. One, mentioned in the Ten Commandments, states: "For in six days the Lord made heaven and earth, the sea, and all that is in them, and rested on the seventh day; wherefore, the Lord blessed the Sabbath and hallowed it." The second reason given in the Torah is to remind us that God delivered our ancestors from Egypt, where they were held in bondage and were given no rest. The Torah commands us: "And thou shalt remember that thou was a servant in the land of Egypt, and the Lord Thy God commanded thee to keep the Sabbath Day."

Thus, Shabbat conveys to us a twofold lesson. One stresses the great religious truth that God created the world and that the universe is not the result of chance or accident but is the work of a divine, intelligent power. The second makes us aware of God as the redeemer of Israel from bondage.

These motives indicate that Shabbat is both Jewish and universal in character. Shabbat makes the Jew aware that God redeemed his or her ancestors from slavery and transformed them into a great and free people. Shabbat also teaches us that God is the Creator of the world and the source of life and of all human blessings. These truths taught by Shabbat are of deep concern to Jew and non-Jew alike. They affirm that all men, regardless of their station in life or their religious and racial origins, are free and equal before God. Even the animals in our employ and nature are included in this divine gift of rest and peace.

Shabbat as a Day of Rest

The foremost law pertaining to the observance of Shabbat is expressed in the biblical command: "Thou shalt do no manner of work." The Jew is commanded that every member of his family including his servant and his animals must abstain from all types of labor. While the Torah does not give a definition of the term labor, the Talmud explains it to be acts such as cooking, kindling fire, and traveling beyond a certain distance. As a general rule, the work prohibited on Shabbat can be divided into two categories:

These truths taught by Shabbat are of deep concern to Jew and non-Jew alike. They affirm that all men, regardless of their station in life or their religious and racial origins, are free and equal before God. Even the animals in our employ and nature are included in this divine gift of rest and peace.

a) Any act which is regarded as labor in the Bible or Talmud. The *Mishnah* (the first section of the Talmud) enumerates thirty-nine classes of labor which are forbidden on Shabbat. Among these are plowing, sowing, reaping, writing, cooking, hunting, killing of animals, kindling fire, building, and business transactions.

b) "Lighter" types of labor or acts which do not entail any manner of work, but that are also forbidden by the rabbis of the Talmud. The reasons for forbidding these less laborious acts is that such performances might ultimately lead to the violation of Shabbat laws or the disturbance of Shabbat rest.

Mention should be made that transgression of Shabbat laws is permitted and even mandatory when human life or health are at stake (for the sake of *piku'ach nefesh*). This is based on the principle that one of the main purposes of the Torah is to help preserve life and promote human welfare. A religious person is, therefore, urged to desecrate the Sabbath laws for the sake of one who is seriously sick. This is also in agreement with the opinions expressed in the Talmud that human life is as holy as the Sabbath and that "the Sabbath was created for sake of Israel and not Israel for the sake of the Sabbath."

Shabbat as a Day of Joy

Unlike the pagan day of rest, the Jewish Shabbat is a day of delight, joyous relaxation, and simple pleasures. It is not to be a day of sadness or austerity. Anything that might mar the cheer and brightness of the day is banned.

While some ancient peoples like the Babylonians and Egyptians had a day resembling Shabbat, it differed basically from that of the Jews. Theirs was mainly a day of gloom and ill luck, abounding in many superstitious beliefs. Unlike the pagan day of rest, the Jewish Shabbat is a day of delight, joyous relaxation, and simple pleasures. It is not to be a day of sadness or austerity. Anything that might mar the cheer and brightness of the day is banned. Neither mourning nor fasting is permitted on Shabbat. Furthermore, for married couples it is considered a *mitzvah* to have sex on Shabbat.

Shabbat as Day of Worship and Study

By far, the most significant purpose of Shabbat is to make life holy, to bring man closer to God and to the teachings of the Jewish faith. The rabbis of the Talmud clearly defined this objective when they affirmed that Shabbat was to be utilized "half for yourself and half for God." They implied thereby that the day was to be observed not merely as one of rest and relaxation but as a day dedicated to worship, study and to the higher interests of life.

The solemnity of the day descends upon the community as the worshippers assemble in the synagogue Friday evening to welcome the "Shabbat Queen" with prayers and hymns of praise. The *Ma'ariv* or *Erev Shabbat* service is preceded by the recitation of psalms known as *Kabbalat Shabbat*. These psalms are followed by a Shabbat hymn, *"Lecha Dodi."* The refrain of this hymn is "Come, my friend, to welcome the bride of Shabbat," depicting the relationship between the Jewish people and Shabbat as one of love, the Jewish people being the groom, Shabbat being the bride. At the conclusion of the evening services the cantor chants the *Kiddush* for those who have no family to share Shabbat with or home to celebrate Shabbat at.

On the Sabbath day the synagogue is not only a house of prayer but also a focal point for study and cultural endeavors. During the morning services the worshipper hears the reading of the weekly portion from the Torah, the *Sidrah* (or *Parasha*), and from the prophetical writings, the *Haftorah*, and he or she is educated by comments of his rabbi who expounded on these texts. The yearly cycle of Torah reading is divided into 54 parts and is universal throughout the Jewish world.

In the afternoon the synagogue is a center of educational activity that is designed to cater to the cultural needs of the more scholarly as well as to the less educated. In the old days (and still in Orthodox circles) it was mostly men who flocked to the synagogue prior to the *Minchah* service for religious instruction in the various branches of Jewish knowledge. Some joined groups engaged in the study of the weekly portion of the Torah and the rabbinic commentaries pertaining to it. Others perused selections from the Talmud and *Midrash* that are full of beautiful legends and moral teachings designed to guide one in daily life. Those who were not inclined to study a religious text derived pleasure from listening to the preacher whose sermon and popular appeal offered the listener an inspiring religious message.

On the Sabbath day the synagogue is not only a house of prayer but also a focal point for study and cultural endeavors.

Shabbat in the Home and Synagogue

Shabbat starts at sundown on Friday night. In the days when the roles in the family were less emancipated than they are now, but still even today in traditional circles, creating Shabbat at home rested upon the wife. Creating Shabbat at home means shopping for the best food of the week and the preparation of a festive meal. The *challot* (Shabbat loaves) have to be baked. They serve as a reminder of the double portion of manna which the children of Israel gathered every Friday. The Shabbat table is usually set with white cloth, candleholders, a bottle of wine or grape juice and a *Kiddush* cup. The two *challot* covered with an embroidered napkin.

Shabbat begins as the mother kindles the lights and recites the appropriate blessing, adding a personal prayer for her family. The father blesses the children and chants the *Kiddush*, the prayer recited over the goblet of wine which emphasizes the holiness of the day. The *challot* are cut and given to each member of the family after which the *Hamotzi* blessing is pronounced. The meal is served with characteristic Shabbat dishes. Between the courses *Zemirot* (religious hymns and songs of thanksgiving) are sung. The meal is concluded with the recitation of grace, called the *Birkat Hamazon*. Although many families have developed their own Shabbat rituals, the most important thing may not be the rituals themselves, but rather having valuable time as a family together, something which is becoming scarcer and scarcer in modern-day life.

The service on Saturday morning is chanted in a special Shabbat melody. The Torah scroll is taken out and the weekly portion, the *Sidrah*, is read. Seven members of the congregation are called up to the Torah, which is called an *Aliyah*, and two more receive the honor of lifting and dressing the scroll. The last, and often the most coveted *Aliyah*, is the privilege of chanting from the *Haftorah*, the weekly section from the prophetical writings which is customarily offered to a *Bar Mitzvah* boy or a bridegroom. Immediately following the Torah reading the rabbi preaches the sermon on the weekly *Sidrah*.

The noon meal at home begins with a brief *Kiddush*. The food prepared the day before and the favorite Shabbat dishes are served. The *Zemirot* are sung and grace is chanted.

Although many families have developed their own Shabbat rituals, the most important thing may not be the rituals themselves, but rather having valuable time as a family together, something which is becoming scarcer and scarcer in modern-day life.

The End of Shabbat: The *Havdalah* Ceremony

Just as Shabbat begins with the ceremony of candles and *Kiddush*, it is closed with the performance of a ceremony called *Havdalah*. "Havdalah" means "distinction" and the purpose of this ceremony is to distinguish between the holiness of Shabbat and the weekdays. Jewish Law requires that such formal separation is made and that no work is permitted on Saturday before dark until the *Havdalah* prayer is recited.

The father begins the *Havdalah* ceremony by reciting a blessing over a goblet of wine or any other beverage, except water. He also recites a blessing over spices which are contained in an artistically designed spice box of metal or wood and over the light of a twisted candle, held by a child. As each of the respective blessings are said, he inhales the fragrance of the spices as to let the sweet smell of Shabbat linger a little longer and brings his hands toward the light of the candle, enabling him to distinguish between light and darkness. The blessing over the light is to thank God for the creation of light and fire. And as the family bids farewell to Shabbat by means of the *Havdalah* prayer, they offer gratitude to God for the joyfulness of the day and voice their yearning for life's blessing of health, peace, and happiness. The ceremony concludes with the greeting "*Shavua Tov*" ("May it be a good week for us and for all Israel.").

Just as Shabbat begins with the ceremony of candles and **Kiddush,** *it is closed with the performance of a ceremony called* **Havdalah.**

Rosh HaShanah

The main purpose of the Jewish religion is to keep people on the path of righteous conduct and moral living. But since we can fail and have a tendency to yield to unworthy desires, we often divert from the right course that Judaism has set for us. That's why Judaism has developed a unique institution known as the Ten Days of Repentance. This period was developed to assist man in returning to the path of upright living and to bring him in harmony with himself and the world around him.

These *Yamim Nora'im* (Days of Awe) start with *Rosh HaShanah*, the Jewish New Year, and reach a climax on *Yom Kippur*, the Day of Atonement. These are the holiest days on the Jewish calendar. With the approach of the Ten Days of Repentance, the religious Jew becomes aware that the day of judgment is drawing near and that soon he will be called upon to stand

The main purpose of the Jewish religion is to keep people on the path of righteous conduct and moral living.

before the Divine Judge to give a full account of his life and conduct over the past year. He also realizes the serious nature of those days which are devoted to prayer, seeking forgiveness of sin, and attempts to improve his way of life. These Holy Days hold a message of hope that the gates of repentance are open to all who have gone astray and that God, our Merciful Father, is ready to forgive those who truly seek to return to Him.

Rosh HaShanah and *Yom Kippur* differ from the other Jewish festivals (*Pesach, Shavuot* and *Sukkot*) in that they have no agricultural or historical meaning. They do not commemorate events that occurred in the early history of our people. They are concerned only with the religious and moral affairs of the individual, dealing only with his personal conduct and with matters of conscience.

Rosh HaShanah *and Yom Kippur *do not commemorate events that occurred in the early history of our people. They are concerned only with the religious and moral affairs of the individual, dealing only with his personal conduct and with matters of conscience.

The following names of the Jewish New Year describe the purpose and the message which it aims to convey:

Rosh HaShanah, meaning "the beginning of the year," is the most familiar name of the festival. The Jewish New Year occurs on the first and second day of *Tishri*, the seventh month on the Jewish calendar. According to the rabbis of the Talmud, the first day of *Tishri* marks the Creation of the World.

Day of Judgment. On this day, according to the words of the Talmud, "all people pass before God in judgment like sheep before the Shepherd." On this day God pronounces judgment on all His creatures who are held acceptable for their deeds and behavior.

Day of Remembrance. God remembers man's deeds and thoughts and deals with him in mercy and truth. On this day the Jew is called upon to remember the beginning of the world and the crucial events in the early history of his or her people. He or she must also remember his or her duties to God and to obey His commandments.

Day of Sounding the *Shofar*. This is the oldest name of the holiday. The *Shofar*, made of ram's horn is one of the most important symbols connected with the observance of *Rosh HaShanah*. The ceremony of blowing the *Shofar* takes place in the synagogue during the morning services. This ceremony is omitted if the first day of the New Year occurs on the Shabbat. An atmosphere of awe and silent reverence descends when this ancient ritual is performed. To Jews of all ages the sounds of the *Shofar* constitute a call to conscience, to repent for their misdeeds and to return to God, to goodness, to others... and to themselves. This returning is called *teshuvah*.

The New Year is ushered in at sunset of the preceding day with the lighting of the holiday candles and the reciting of the *Rosh HaShanah Kiddush*. There are many customs expressing the wish for a good and sweet year. Ashkenazim dip a slice of apple into honey. Moroccan Jews eat slices of carrot (symbolizing money, material wealth) in honey. Another custom is to eat the head of a fish, symbolizing the desire to be the head of things to come and not the tail. Everywhere in the world worshippers greet each other in the synagogue with the words *"L'Shanah Tova Tikotevu"* ("May you be inscribed for a good year") at the evening *Rosh HaShanah* service.

The synagogue services on the day of *Rosh HaShanah* begin early in the morning and end after midday. The prayers that are recited stand out for their sublime teachings and universal appeal. They deal with the worshipper's personal needs, expressing his or her plans for life, health and prosperity; they voice the Jewish yearning for peace, justice and brotherhood. Worshippers pray to God to hasten the day when the mighty shall be just and he righteous triumphant; when arrogance and wickedness of nations shall vanish like smoke. This grand vision about the future of mankind is contained in the *Aleinu* prayer, which is part of the *Rosh HaShanah Amidah* service. This prayer affirms that it is the duty of the Jewish people to proclaim the Kingship of God unto all peoples. It voices the hope that the day will come "When all nations will acknowledge God as the Supreme Ruler of the World."

Musaf, the additional service, stresses three important ideas. It aims to impress the following basic beliefs upon the worshipper: the greatness and majesty of God, the sinfulness and the moral weakness of man, and the ability of man to rise above his moral deficiencies and failings by trying to govern his life in accordance with God's will. The *Musaf* service of the *Rosh HaShanah Amidah* is divided into three parts. The first, known as *Malchuyot*, proclaims God as the Creator and Ruler of the world, to whom every creature is responsible. The second section, *Zichronot*, describes God as remembering the world and as the Judge of every human being and his actions.

The prayers that are recited stand out for their sublime teachings and universal appeal. They deal with the worshipper's personal needs, expressing his or her plans for life, health and prosperity; they voice the Jewish yearning for peace, justice and brotherhood.

The third part, *Shofar*, recalls God as the Lawgiver who revealed Himself at Mt. Sinai and gave the Torah to Israel accompanied by the blasts of the *Shofar*.

The most widely known prayer, recited both on *Rosh HaShanah* and *Yom Kippur* is *Unetaneh Tokef*. This religious poem describes the Day of Judgment when God sits upon His throne to judge every human being and decrees the person's fate during the coming year. This prayer makes the worshipper aware that during these High Holy Days God decides "Who shall live and who shall die, who prosper and shall grow poor, who shall have rest and peace and shall wander." Yet, at the conclusion of this prayer, he is offered the comforting hope that, "repentance, prayer, and charity can avert the decree."

This implies that man possesses the power to undo the evil consequences of his past behavior. This prayer emphasizes one of the great teachings of the Jewish religion: Man is not a helpless puppet in the hands of fate, but is a free agent. He can be the master of his destiny in matters of personal conduct and character. He possesses inner resources to overcome the impulse to do evil and he can change the future by changing himself.

Although some interpret the idea of judgment literally, others understand it as a matter of conscience.

Although some interpret the idea of judgment literally, others understand it as a matter of conscience. Here we see a fundamental difference with Christianity. Where prayer literally means "petition," the Hebrew word for prayer, *lehitpalel*, means "to judge oneself." Similarly, the Hebrew word for "sin," *chet*, means "to miss the mark." Judaism emphasizes free will so much that, as a consequence, we may hurt others and others may hurt us while exercising the ability to choose. With our free will, we at times make choices that could have been better, we "miss the mark." When we pray, we examine how we have exercised our free will and where and when we have missed the mark.

In contrast with the Christian concept of original sin, Judaism see human behavior as the result of human nature, which has both good and bad inclinations.

In contrast with the Christian concept of original sin, Judaism see human behavior as the result of human nature, which has both good and bad inclinations. Humankind is not exclusively "good" or "bad," but a mixture of both. This difference with regard to Christian doctrine may seem subtle, yet it has a major influence on how we look at human potential. Where the belief in original sin can originate a feeling of negativity and impotence, the perspective of being human, being both good and bad, gives us the ability to fix what we feel is not working inside of us. Second, if the choices we make are subordinated to original sin, an entity outside of ourselves must save us when we make the wrong choices. For Christianity, this entity is Jesus: only those who believe in him are saved. For Judaism, our relationship with God is direct and personal, resulting in a personal responsibility for our salvation.

On *Rosh HaShanah*, the idea of personal responsibility for salvation is expressed in introspection as a psychologically therapeutic resource, and in repentance (*teshuvah*). We judge our lives and we repent, we "return." After introspection and repentance, we are renewed. This renewal is the key to this holiday, a holiday that affirms life, that reminds us of the potential we have in ourselves for perfection, as we are created in God's image.

Yom Kippur

A mood of awe and solemnity is also felt during the days after the New Year, the Ten Days of Repentance which have additional prayers of repentance added to the daily liturgy. The Ten Days of Repentance reach a climax on *Yom Kippur*, the Day of Atonement, which occurs on the tenth of *Tishri*.

The whole period of the High Holidays is focused on repentance, on repairing ourselves and our position in the world. Where the holidays of *Rosh HaShanah* and *Yom Kippur* take place at the synagogue and concentrate on our relationship with God, the ten intermediate days are for our relationships with our fellow human beings. Just as we ask God for forgiveness on *Rosh HaShanah* and *Yom Kippur* for any of our sins and transgressions committed against Him, we ought to use the Ten Days of Repentance to ask our fellow human beings for forgiveness.

According to Judaism, there are two types of sins. There are transgressions one commits against God. We sin against God when we disobey His commands and perform acts that are contrary to God's will. When we ignore or violate the basic laws and religious observances, decreed in the Torah and in the Talmud and developed by later rabbinical authorities, and which were handed down from one generation to another, these are transgressions committed directly against God.

Then there are sins we commit against our fellow man by disobeying the laws of moral conduct. When we fail to observe the rules of righteous living by dealing unjustly and dishonestly with our fellow men; when we

*On **Rosh HaShanah**, the idea of personal responsibility for salvation is expressed in introspection as a psychologically therapeutic resource, and in repentance (teshuvah).*

The whole period of the High Holidays is focused on repentance, on repairing ourselves and our position in the world.

deceive our neighbors or business associates, damage their possessions, injure their welfare and hurt their reputations, nurse a grudge against them or humiliate then in the presence of others, any one of these acts is labeled by Judaism as a sin committed both against man and, indirectly, against God.

We commit these sins indirectly against God for two reasons. It is God who gave us the laws of moral conduct and the idea that every human being is created in the image of God. However, it is not up to God to forgive us these sins, as we only indirectly transgressed against him. With our personal responsibility for salvation we can only be forgiven by those against whom we have sinned. Not until we have tried to reestablish friendly relations between them and ourselves, we have called upon relatives, friends and neighbors to ask forgiveness for wrongs we have committed with or without intention, we have offered good wishes for the New Year, and have made customary donations to charitable purposes, are we spiritually prepared for *Yom Kippur*.

Yom Kippur, described in the Bible as "The Shabbat," is the major fast and holiest day in the Jewish calendar. On this day one must abstain from food, drink, and other physical stimuli from sunset to sunset. All work and normal occupations are forbidden. Services in the synagogue, beginning at sunset, continue the next morning throughout the day without interruption until dusk. It is a day when Jews withdraw from worldly interests and material pursuits and devote themselves exclusively to their spiritual needs and to the higher goals of life. They spend the entire day in prayer and meditation. They confess their sins and fervently plead that God forgive them their transgressions. They firmly resolve to abandon their sinful conduct, to cleanse their hearts of moral impurities, and to become reconciled with God.

The day preceding the Day of Atonement, known as *Erev Yom Kippur*, is crowded with the observance of customs and practices which aim to prepare us emotionally for this sacred day. The meal proceeding the fast is eaten before sundown and, according to the Talmud, it is as much a duty to partake of this meal as it is to fast on *Yom Kippur*.

After the meal the mother kindles the usual festival lights and the father lights memorial candles, which burn for 24 hours in memory of departed parents.

With our personal responsibility for salvation we can only be forgiven by those against whom we have sinned.

Yom Kippur, described in the Bible as "The Shabbat," is the major fast and holiest day in the Jewish calendar.

The holiest day of the year is ushered in as the community assembles in the synagogue for the evening service. White, the symbol of purity, is the dominant color on *Yom Kippur*. The ark cover and Torah mantles are changed to white. The rabbi and cantor are also attired in white robes and many men wear white skull caps. The uniqueness of this evening service is emphasized when the Torah scrolls are taken from the ark and are handed to the elders of the congregation. These men hold the scrolls and all stand alongside the cantor, who begins to chant the *Kol Nidre* prayer.

Kol Nidre, meaning "all vows," is really more than a prayer. It is actually a legal formula whereby man declares all vows, promises, or oaths which he made to God and neglected to fulfill, null and void. He, therefore, petitions God to release him from the vows and promises, which he made in moments of great anger or grief or when under unusual pressure, and which could not be carried out. The rabbis of the Talmud stressed that this formula of annulment only deals with sins committed against God and refers to vows that are purely personal and religious, for, they affirm, no prayer can absolve man from pledges and obligations he made to his fellow man. Despite this affirmation, this aspect of Judaism has been frequently used by anti-Semites to disseminate their hatred of Judaism, by stating that the *Kol Nidre* formula is proof of the fact that the promises or oaths Jews make to non-Jews are void by a religious conspiracy.

One can obtain a full appreciation of this holiest day in the Jewish year by examining the great message it proclaims and the eternal moral teaching and beliefs which its prayers voice so eloquently. One of the most important teachings of Judaism seen in the prayers of *Yom Kippur* is the belief that, while man is accountable for his actions, God grants him every opportunity to repent and that the doors to repentance are open to all.

Man need not be crushed by the burden of his sins and wrongdoings; he can, if he desires, shake off its yoke. Man is a free agent, and if he tries hard enough, he can overcome his evil habits and check his inclinations to do wrong. He alone can decide whether or not he will be a decent and righteous individual. The prayers of the day dwell continuously on the meaning and purpose of repentance. They indicate to the worshipper the steps he or she must take on the road leading to full atonement and forgiveness of sin.

One of the most important teachings of Judaism seen in the prayers of Yom Kippur *is the belief that, while man is accountable for his actions, God grants him every opportunity to repent and that the doors to repentance are open to all.*

The first step in the process of repentance is to acknowledge one's sins and express sincere regret and remorse for past actions. But being sorry for wrongs done is not enough. One must break with the past; whenever possible, try to undo the harmful consequences of his wrongdoing and seek forgiveness from God or from the person against whom he sinned. But the most important step the repentant sinner must take is to resolve firmly not to repeat his or her sinful acts. Sincere repentance demands not only avoiding evil, but seeking to do good and to live in harmony with God's will. This is how one can attain the goal of atonement, to be at-one-with-God.

Since the confession of sins is the main theme of *Yom Kippur*, the confessional prayer stands out as a distinctive feature of the services. The confessional, which begins with *Al Chet* ("For the sin...") is included in each of the five services of *Yom Kippur*. It enumerates the moral offenses of which one may be guilty and asks for pardon and forgiveness. Among the listed sins are: arrogance, cruelty, dishonesty, greed, slander, treachery in dealing with one's neighbors, irresponsibility in speech and though, profanation of God's name and disrespect for parents and elders. Most of these offenses are of the kind one commits against his or her fellow men and are thus also sins against God.

As the confessional is recited in unison by the community, it is unlikely that any single individual has committed all the sins recited in the prayer, yet it is very possible that, among all the congregants, most of the sins have been committed. This reflects Judaism's ethical commitment to community. Together we ask for forgiveness for all the sins, and together, in solidarity, we must try to avoid them being committed. Our responsibility is not limited to ourselves. *Al Chet* is recited publicly in the first person plural ("we"), which underscores not our *guilt* but our *responsibility*. As the Jewish thinker Heschel said, "In a free society some are guilty but all are responsible."

Judaism offers us a few guiding principles to help us understand the nature and meaning of sin and to enable us to decide which of our acts of commission or omission are to be classed as sins. One well-known definition, mentioned in the Talmud, states that any act which causes a man to be estranged from God constitutes a sin. Also, any act that serves to defile man's soul and causes him to decline to a state of unworthiness may be classified as a sin.

Al Chet *is recited publicly in the first person plural ("we"), which underscores not our* guilt *but our* responsibility. *As the Jewish thinker Heschel said, "In a free society some are guilty but all are responsible."*

The prayers of the day of *Yom Kippur* are divided into four distinct services: *Shacharit*, the morning service, *Musaf*, the additional service, *Minchah* the afternoon service, and *Neilah*, the closing service. Each of these includes a confession of sins and prayer for forgiveness. The *Unetaneh Tokef* prayer, which is recited on *Rosh HaShanah*, is also repeated on *Yom Kippur*.

About noon time, immediately following the reading from Scriptures, a memorial service for the deceased is held. At this hour the community lovingly recall the memory of departed parents and close relatives and offers prayer in their behalf. The congregation also recalls with reverence and gratitude the heroes and martyrs of Israel of all generations who were ready to sacrifice their lives for their faith and people.

The concluding service of the day is known as *Neilah*, which is the Hebrew word for "the closing of the gate." Its name is derived from the fact that the gates of the Temple of Jerusalem were closed at the twilight hour. Later, the meaning of the term *Neilah* was extended to refer to the heavenly gates of prayer and repentance which close at the end of *Yom Kippur*, when the fate each individual has been decreed.

This closing service is most impressive, comparable to that of *Kol Nidre*. As the shadows begin to lengthen, the worshippers experience a feeling of urgency because they realize the *Neilah* time represents the last chance for repentance and divine forgiveness. This accounts for the fact that the prayer "inscribe us in the book of life," used throughout the Ten Days of Penitence, is now changed to "seal us in the book of life."

As the evening twilight turns into night, the service reaches an impressive climax when the entire congregation recites in unison and with great fervor the opening sentence of the *Sh'ma*. "Praise be the name of His glorious Kingdom forever and ever" is repeated three times and seven times the phrase, "The Lord, He is God," is exclaimed. A long blast of the *Shofar* is sounded before the open ark, while the congregation stands in reverence, proclaiming that the Fast of *Yom Kippur* is ended.

The duty to fast on *Yom Kippur* stands out as one of the prominent observances of the day. The Bible clearly states the commandment, "The tenth day of the seventh month is a day of atonement (...) You shall afflict your souls."

A long blast of the Shofar is sounded before the open ark, while the congregation stands in reverence, proclaiming that the Fast of Yom Kippur is ended. The duty to fast on Yom Kippur stands out as one of the prominent observances of the day.

Ancient religions regarded the practice of fasting as a way to torment the body in order to help man to win the favor of his pagan gods. In the Jewish religion, however, the primary purpose of fasting was to discipline the body and soul. The ancient teachers of Judaism maintained that when man tries to curb his physical appetites and refuses to satisfy the cravings of his body he is drawn closer to the spiritual ideals of life. They believe that the experience of hunger and weakness gives one a sense of humility and directs his attention to the needs of the soul and to serious thoughts on life. It can help him understand the following truth expressed in the Torah, "Man does not live by bread alone but by everything that comes out of the mouth of the Lord." Fasting is an instrument that helps us in our introspection and reflection. It is a symbolic (and real) cleansing of the mind and body, a way of affirming our control over our selves, as well as of exercising our freedom, since we remember that others fast because they have no choice, but we are fortunate to have such a choice. Therefore, we are not exempt from sharing the responsibility for this fact. Hence, many choose to give more *tzeddakah* on *Yom Kippur*. Fasting is, then, a cleansing, but also an awakening of the conscience.

Fasting is an instrument that helps us in our introspection and reflection. It is a symbolic (and real) cleansing of the mind and body, a way of affirming our control over our selves, as well as of exercising our freedom, since we remember that others fast because they have no choice, but we are fortunate to have such a choice.

Pilgrimage festivals

The Jewish calendar knows three festivals which coincide with three periods of harvest in Israel. The Bible proscribed that everyone in Israel was obliged to bring offerings of the harvest to the Temple in Jerusalem; hence, the name "Pilgrimage Festivals," as everybody made pilgrimage to Jerusalem to fulfill the Biblical commandment.

Two of the three festivals have a great influence on American culture. *Sukkot*, which celebrates the abundance of the fall harvest, inspired Thanksgiving. *Pesach*, with its message of freedom that resonates strongly with the American culture, is often celebrated in an interfaith setting these days, an initiative of Christian churches who invite their Jewish neighbors to share the universal humanitarian concepts of the holiday.

Sukkot

The holiday of *Sukkot* ("Booths") celebrates the abundance of the fall harvest. While originally a purely biblical agricultural festival with the name of *Chag HaAsif*, the "Festival of Ingathering," we now commemorate the forty-year period during which the children of Israel were wandering in the desert, living in temporary shelters.

Sukkot starts five days after *Yom Kippur*, on the fifteenth of the Hebrew month of *Tishri*, and lasts for seven days. Traditionally, one starts to build a booth, the holiday's most significant feature, immediately after finishing the meal that breaks the *Yom Kippur* fast. There is probably no better example of the Jewish emphasis on action than this custom, as a period of spirituality is directly followed by immersion in the material world by actual physical labor. It is just as telling for Jewish tradition that this festival is also referred to as *Zeman Simchateinu*, the "Season of our Rejoicing," a period of solemn introspection directly followed by a period of open joy. Actually, this is the only festival where the Bible tells us in so many words to be happy and rejoice.

In honor of the holiday's historical significance, we are commanded to dwell in temporary shelters, as our ancestors did in the wilderness. The commandment to "dwell" in a *sukkah* can be fulfilled by simply eating all of one's meals there; however, if the weather, climate, and one's health permit, one should live in the *sukkah* as much as possible, including sleeping in it. A *sukkah* must have at least three walls covered with a material that will not blow away in the wind. A *sukkah* may be any size, so long as it is large enough for you to fulfill the commandment of dwelling in it. The roof of the *sukkah* must be made of material that grew from the ground and was cut off, such as tree branches, corn stalks, bamboo reeds, or sticks. The covering must be left loose, not tied together or tied down, and must allow rain to get in. When dwelling in the *sukkah* at night, one has to be able to look through the openings in the roof and see the stars. The lack of protection against the elements makes us aware of the true message of *Sukkot*: As human beings we are vulnerable and for real protection and sustenance we will never be able to fully rely on the material world. Only God can give us protection and sustenance.

Building and decorating a *sukkah* is a fun, family project, much like decorating the Christmas tree is for Christians. Many Americans remark on how much the *sukkah* (and the holiday generally) reminds them of Thanksgiving.

Sukkot *starts five days after* Yom Kippur, *on the fifteenth of the Hebrew month of* Tishri, *and lasts for seven days.*

Building and decorating a sukkah *is a fun, family project, much like decorating the Christmas tree is for Christians.*

This is not entirely coincidental. Our American pilgrims, who created the Thanksgiving holiday, were deeply religious people. When they were trying to find a way to express their thanks for their survival and for the harvest, they looked to the Bible for an appropriate way of celebrating and based their celebration in part on *Sukkot*.

Another observance related to *Sukkot* involves what are known as "The Four Species" (*arba minim*), or the *lulav* and *etrog*. We are commanded to take these four plants and use them to "rejoice before the L-rd." The four species in question are a citrus fruit native to Israel (*etrog*), a palm branch (*lulav*), two willow branches (*arava*) and three myrtle branches (*hadas*). The six branches are bound together and referred to collectively as the *lulav*. The *etrog* is held separately. With these four species in hand, one recites a blessing and waves the species in all six directions (east, south, west, north, up and down, symbolizing the fact that God is everywhere).

Shemini Atzeret and Simchat Torah

*On **Tishri 22, the day after the seventh day of** Sukkot, **the holiday** Shemini Atzeret **is celebrated.***

On *Tishri* 22, the day after the seventh day of *Sukkot*, the holiday *Shemini Atzeret* is celebrated. In Israel *Shemini Atzeret* is also the holiday of *Simchat Torah*. Outside of Israel only the second day of *Shemini Atzeret* is *Simchat Torah*. Although these two holidays are technically not pilgrimage festivals, they are so interwoven with the celebrations of *Sukkot* that they are seen as an integral part of *Sukkot*.

Shemini Atzeret literally means "the assembly of the eighth (day)." Rabbinic literature explains the holiday this way: God is like a host, who invites us as visitors for the week of *Sukkot*, but when the time comes for us to leave, He has enjoyed Himself so much that He asks us to stay another day.

The annual cycle of weekly Torah readings is completed at this time of year. We read the last Torah portion, then proceed immediately to the first chapter of Genesis, reminding us that the Torah is a circle, and never ends.

The annual cycle of weekly Torah readings is completed at this time of year. We read the last Torah portion, then proceed immediately to the first chapter of Genesis, reminding us that the Torah is a circle, and never ends. This completion and simultaneous recommencement of the readings is a time of great celebration. This holiday is known as *Simchat Torah*, which means "Rejoicing of the Law."

Pesach

Pesach, Festival of Freedom, born of the liberation from Egyptian bondage, has left an indelible impression on Jewish memory. Research show that unaffiliated Jews are more likely to celebrate *Pesach* as an expression of their heritage than the High Holidays. Apart from its observance in the synagogue, *Pesach* has a unique place in the Jewish home because of the *Seder* and because of the changed atmosphere in the home during the Passover week. The Passover home atmosphere is created by the traditional practice of thoroughly cleansing the home to remove all *chametz* ("leaven"), whose use is meticulously avoided throughout the Passover days. The term *chametz* is applied not only to foods, but also to the dishes and utensils in which foods are prepared or served during the rest of the year and which may not be used during *Pesach*.

The feast of Passover begins on the 15th day of *Nisan* and lasts eight days. Only the first two and the last two days are holy days; the four middle days are called "*Chol HaMoed*," the ordinary days of the festival. The festival is known as the "Season of our Freedom" because it commemorates the emancipation of our ancestors from Egyptian slavery. It is also designated as "*Chag HaMatzot*," or the "Feast of the Unleavened Bread," reminding us that in the miraculous departure from Egypt there was no time for the dough to ferment, and it had to be prepared in a hurry. The word "*Pesach*" means "to pass over" and it reminds us that God smote all the first born of the Egyptians, but passed over the houses of the Israelites.

Below is a short list of Passover terms and concepts:

Seder: Literally means "order," referring to the order of how the *Pesach* story is to be recalled on the first and second night of *Pesach*, as prescribed in the *Haggadah*.

Haggadah: A Hebrew word meaning a "story." The *Haggadah* read at the *Seder* contains the story of the miserable life of the ancient Hebrews in Egypt and how they were freed from slavery. It also contains many beautiful prayers, hymns, and songs which are read and sung at the *Seder*.

Matzah: The unleavened bread or the bread of affliction reminds us of the hardships that our fathers endured in Egypt, and of the haste with which they departed the house of slavery.

Pesach, Festival of Freedom, born of the liberation from Egyptian bondage, has left an indelible impression on Jewish memory.

The feast of Passover begins on the 15th day of Nisan and lasts eight days.

Maror: The horseradish symbolizing the bitter life of the enslaved Israelites in Egypt.

Charoset: A mixture consisting of nuts, apples, wine, and cinnamon (according to the Ashkenazi recipe, there are many variations) chopped and ground together, representing the mortar and clay which the Jews used in making bricks as slaves in Egypt.

Carpas, **or parsley:** Made part of the meal to signify a festive supper as befits a great occasion. The purpose of dipping it in salt water is to make it palatable.

Dipping: At one time the parsley is dipped into salt water; at another time the *maror* is dipped in *charoset*. The salt water represents the Red Sea and the miracle associated with it. Some say it represents the tears which the Jews shed in bondage.

Roasted shank bone: A symbol of the paschal lamb, the sacrifices of which was the central feature of the Passover celebration during the existence of the Temple.

Roasted egg A symbol of the burnt offering brought on every day of the feast in the days of the Temple in Jerusalem.

Reclining: Traditionally, the master of the house leans on a pillow, toward the left, during the *Seder* service. This is a position symbolic of freedom, since slaves were never permitted such a luxury.

The cup of Elijah: Jewish tradition pictures the prophet Elijah as the forerunner of the coming of the Messiah, who will redeem Israel from its present plight and who will establish the kingdom of God on Earth. This night recalls both Israel's past redemption and hope for the future. Hence, a cup is designated as the cup of Elijah. Incidentally, this is a symbol of warm hospitality extended to strangers in every Jewish home on *Seder* night.

The opening of the door: Some explain it to refer to the expectation of the visit of Elijah in every Jewish home, to herald good news of Israel's redemption. Others explain it as an expression of the justified anger of the Jews against those who spread the malicious lie that the blood of Gentiles is used in the *Seder* ceremonies.

Afikoman: A Greek word meaning "dessert." In Temple days, the meal would finish with the meat of the paschal lamb. In our days, we make the

Jewish tradition pictures the prophet Elijah as the forerunner of the coming of the Messiah, who will redeem Israel from its present plight and who will establish the kingdom of God on Earth.

matzah the official dessert of the *Seder* meal. To keep the children alert during the *Seder*, the *afikoman* is hidden at the beginning of the *Seder*. The children try to find it and take it when the father is unaware. At the end of the *Seder* when the *afikoman* is to be eaten, the father redeems it by promising some gift in return for it.

The four cups: The four cups represent the four promises for redemption made by God to Israel. Each cup has a specific place in the service. The first serves as *Kiddush*; the second is taken at the conclusion of the first part of the *Seder*; the third is taken at the conclusion of grace recited after the meal; the fourth cup comes at the conclusion of the *Seder*.

Food prohibited during *Pesach*: Leavened bread, cakes, biscuits and crackers, cereals, coffee substances derived from cereals, wheat, barley, oats, rice, dry beans, and all liquids which contain ingredients or flavors made from grain alcohol. This distinction between what is leavened and what is unleavened food, however, only applies to products that are made out of the following five kinds of grain: barley, wheat, rye, oats, and spelt. It's not that any of these grains are unsuitable for *Pesach* food, it depends on how the products are prepared. If the dough containing any of these five grains is baked immediately after preparation, without any possibility for fermentation, the product is considered unleavened or *matzah* and "*Kosher L'Pesach*." Fermentation of grapes or other fruit does not constitute *chametz* and its use is therefore permitted on *Pesach*.

Permitted foods: The following foods require no "*Kosher L'Pesach*" label and are permitted in unopened packages or containers: natural coffee, sugar, tea, salt, pepper, vegetables. If certified for Passover use by rabbinical authority, one may consume: *matzot*, *matzah* flour, Passover noodles, candies, cakes, beverages, canned and processed foods, milk, butter, jams, cheese, jellies, relishes, dried fruits, frozen fruits and vegetables, salad oils, vegetable gelatin, shortenings, vinegar, wine, and liquors.

The clearing out of *chametz*: All *chametz* is to be cleared out of the house the day before Passover. The official ceremony of clearing out the *chametz* usually takes place the night preceding the first *Seder*, the evening of the 14th of *Nisan*. This ceremony is the climax of the Passover preparation. It should be done in the presence of the whole family and can be made im-

All chametz is to be cleared out of the house the day before Passover. The official ceremony of clearing out the chametz usually takes place the night preceding the first Seder, the evening of the 14th of Nisan.

pressive when the head of the family goes about with a candle in hand and gathers up the crumbs of bread which have been conspicuously placed in different parts of the house. These are gathered and, in a service which is found on the first page of any *Haggadah*, the master of the house renounces possession of all *chametz* which may have remained in the house unknown to him. The ceremony is based on the biblical command which states that "No *chametz* is to be seen in all your borders" during Passover. No *chametz* may be eaten after 10:00 in the morning of *Erev Pesach*.

Here are some tips which will help you make your *Seder* successful:

1. Make sure everyone has the same *Haggadah*. It is fine for two people to share a *Haggadah*. There are many beautiful *Haggadot* now on the market and you have a wide choice.

2. Don't feel that your *Seder* must be too formal. You may interpolate your own comments into the various parts of the service. You may ask others to do the same. Keep the service moving along, but don't feel that it has quite the same formality as a synagogue service. The *Seder* is a unique admixture of the solemn and the joyful.

3. Study the *Haggadah* before the night of the *Seder*. Decide in advance which parts you can do in Hebrew and which in English. Be familiar with the text before you sit down for the ceremony.

4. Rotate the reading of the parts of the *Haggadah* among those at the table. Some will read in English; others in Hebrew. Some will the sing the songs in one style; others will use another melody. The very melange of the Hebrew dialects and the variations in the manner of reading portions of the service will illustrate the diversity of Jewish life and add a special flavor to the proceedings.

5. Have the guests recite as many of the blessings as possible in unison. Some segments can be read in unison so as to encourage the participation of everyone. Traditionally, Passover is a time when you can derive both merriment and inspiration from the great saga of the Exodus. Don't lose the opportunity of introducing the Passover spirit into your own home. You will feel amply rewarded for the little effort entailed.

Traditionally, Passover is a time when you can derive both merriment and inspiration from the great saga of the Exodus. Don't lose the opportunity of introducing the Passover spirit into your own home.

Shavuot

Shavuot (Weeks), is the second of the three major festivals with both historical and agricultural significance and follows exactly 7 weeks, 49 days, after *Pesach*. Agriculturally, it commemorates the time when the first fruits were harvested and brought to the Temple and is known as *Chag HaBikkurim* (the Festival of the First Fruits). Historically, it celebrates the giving of the Torah at Mount Sinai, and is also known as *Chag Matan Torateinu* (the Festival of the Giving of Our Torah). It is noteworthy that the holiday is called the time of the *giving* of the Torah, rather than the time of the *receiving* of the Torah. The sages point out that we are constantly in the process of receiving the Torah, that we receive it every day, but it was first given at this time. Thus, it is the giving, not the receiving, that makes this holiday significant. While *Pesach* celebrates our freedom from physical bondage, it was the giving of the Torah on *Shavuot* that redeemed us spiritually from our bondage to idolatry and immorality.

It is customary to stay up the entire first night of *Shavuot* to study Torah and then pray as early as possible in the morning.

It is customary to eat a dairy meal at least once during *Shavuot*. There are varying opinions as to why this is done. Some say it is a reminder of the promise regarding the land of Israel, a land flowing with "milk and honey." According to another view, it is because our ancestors had just received the Torah (and the dietary laws therein), and did not have both meat and dairy dishes available.

The Book of Ruth is read at this time because the story of Ruth is believed to have taken place around *Shavuot*.

*While **Pesach** celebrates our freedom from physical bondage, it was the giving of the Torah on **Shavuot** that redeemed us spiritually from our bondage to idolatry and immorality.*

Historical Holidays

Not all of Judaism's holidays find their origins in the Bible. Some of the holidays commemorate historical events. The number of historical holidays has significantly increased in recent history with the introduction of holidays like *Yom HaShoah* (Holocaust Memorial Day), *Yom HaAtzma'ut* (Israel's Independence Day) and *Yom Yerushalayim* (Unification of Jerusalem).

Since these new holidays are still in the process of developing their own significance, symbolism, and rituals, it is nearly impossible to give a general

Not all of Judaism's holidays find their origins in the Bible. Some of the holidays commemorate historical events.

and adequate description of their observance. Therefore, this chapter will only concern itself with the more established historical holidays.

Chanukah

When the Greek Empire was split up after the death of Alexander of Macedonia in 323 B.C.E., the rulers of Palestine made continuous attempts to force our people to give up their own faith and to adopt Greek ideas and customs.

When the Greek Empire was split up after the death of Alexander of Macedonia in 323 B.C.E., the rulers of Palestine made continuous attempts to force our people to give up their own faith and to adopt Greek ideas and customs. Although the majority of the people resisted the attempt to divorce them from Judaism, there were some Jewish leaders who helped to introduce pagan practices. However, it was not until the advent, in 175 B.C.E. of King Antiochus in Syria, that force was employed to impose Greek customs and ways of life. This king began to persecute all those Jews who refused to give up the practice of Judaism, he looted the Temple and ordered all Jews to bow down to the idols he placed there.

These acts precipitated an uprising which was led by the Hasmonean family of the little town of *Modi'in*. They were joined by a small, poorly armed band of Jews, zealous about their faith and God, and they were commanded by the Hasmonean Judah, called the Maccabee. After several years of fighting, in which they displayed extraordinary courage and faith, Judah and his men drove the Syrians out. On the 25th of *Kislev,* 165 B.C.E. (exactly three years after the defilement of the Sanctuary), they made their entrance into the Temple and rededicated it to the service of God.

The Talmud records this event thus: "When the Hasmoneans prevailed against the Greeks, they searched the Temple and found only one cruse of oil which lay there untouched and undefiled, intact with the seal of the High Priest. This cruse contained sufficient oil for one day's lighting only; but a miracle was wrought therein, and they lit the lamp with it for eight days. The following year, these days were appointed a festival with the recital of *Hallel* and Thanksgiving." We, therefore, celebrate *Chanukah,* the Festival of Dedication, annually for eight days, beginning on the 25th of *Kislev.*

We celebrate *Chanukah* by kindling the *Chanukiah* for eight nights. Although this candelabrum is generally known as a menorah, this is actually the wrong name for it. A menorah has seven branches symbolizing the seven days of creation, while the candelabrum we use to celebrate *Chanukah* has nine branches, eight for the eight days of the miracle and one called the *Shamash* (guard).

The *Shamash* is not only to light the other candles with, but is also to guard the symbolism of the other candles. The *Chanukah* lights should only symbolize the miracle and not be used for any practical use. Therefore, the *Chanukiah* should be placed so it can't be mistaken for a light that has a practical use. In fact, one should kindle the lights near a window or door in order "to proclaim the miracle."

The time of lighting is immediately at the appearance of the stars; this should not be delayed, and the candles or the oil, either of which may be used, should burn at least half an hour. The order of lighting is as follows: On the first night the candle at the right end of the candelabrum is lit, on the second night an additional light is added to the left and so forth on every consecutive night, with the new candle always the first to be lit.

Chanukah may be particularly recognized as the festival recalling a great act of faith, a feast of dedication commemorating the liberation of our people. It symbolizes the struggles of the "few against the many, the weak against the strong," the eternal battle of the Jewish people for their faith and existence. In short, it symbolizes the fundamental right to *be*. The Jews were not fighting to be like the rest, but for their right to be different. They were fighting, essentially, for a political principle: the idea that a multicultural society should respect, not subordinate, differences. But the historical events also remind us of the importance of Jewish practices or rituals: the king knew that, in order to do away with Judaism, he had first to change what Jews did; by changing what Jews *did* he knew he could change who Jews *were*. Hence, the importance of rituals: it is not always enough to feel Jewish in order to preserve Judaism, in much the same way that a home inhabited by Jews is not the same as a Jewish home. In short, *Chanukah* is a celebration of religious freedom. It is worth mentioning that, until Israeli Independence Day, *Chanukah* was the only celebration of independence for 2,000 years. *Chanukah* reminds us of that oppression as the first historical attempt to eliminate Jewish culture. There had previously been attempts to eliminate Jews, but this time the attempt was to eliminate Judaism itself.

> **Chanukah *symbolizes the struggles of the "few against the many, the weak against the strong," the eternal battle of the Jewish people for their faith and existence. In short, it symbolizes the fundamental right to be. The Jews were not fighting to be like the rest, but for their right to be different.***

Chanukah calls on the world, even today, to remember the eternal message of the prophet Zechariah, read in the *Haftorah* on *Shabbat Chanukah*: "Not by might, nor by power, but by My Spirit, saith the Lord of Hosts." This is a powerful message against violence and for the power of the spirit and of reason. It also explains that, even though in essence *Chanukah* celebrates a military victory, the emphasis of the celebration is focused on the aftermath of this victory, on the spiritual result, the rededication of the Temple.

Purim

Of all the established holidays, *Purim* is without a doubt the most secular recount of Jewish history. The story has no reference to God whatsoever, yet it is understood by all those who participate in the celebration that God's saving power enabled the miraculous twist of events that saved the Jewish people.

The prelude to the story of *Purim* is a lavish banquet held by King Ahashuerus, whose empire extended over 120 provinces, ranging from India to Ethiopia. When the festivities reach their height and the influence of the wine begins to be felt, the King orders Queen Vashti, arrayed in all her beauty, to appear before the vast assembly of noblemen and princes. This the Queen refuses to do. She is deposed, and a search is instituted to find Ahashuerus a new Queen.

The *Purim* story begins with the selection of Esther as the new Queen. Esther is a mysterious Jewess from nowhere, who charms the Emperor with her natural beauty and innate dignity. She is accompanied to the Palace by her uncle Mordechai, a devout Jew.

The story starts to unravel with the introduction of one of the King's ministers by the name of Haman. This figure is the prototypical anti-Semite, bloated with vanity and ordering everybody to bend the knee as he passes by.

When Mordechai refuses to do this for religious reasons (Jews only bend the knee to God, not to any worldly authority), Haman convinces the King that the Jews should be destroyed since they are a subversive power within the Kingdom. From this scene the holiday derives its name, since the day on which the Jews were to be murdered was to be decided by the casting of lots, and *Purim* is the Hebrew word for lots.

This is a powerful message against violence and for the power of the spirit and of reason. It also explains that, even though in essence Chanukah celebrates a military victory, the emphasis of the celebration is focused on the aftermath of this victory, on the spiritual result, the rededication of the Temple.

The story continues with Mordechai learning of the devilish plot of Haman. Mordechai, who always stressed to his niece that she shouldn't reveal her Jewish heritage, now pleads with her to reveal her identity to save her people. Though Esther is daunted by the task at first, she finally decides on a plan that turns out to be as successful as it is ingenious.

Esther invites both the King and Haman to a banquet in her own private apartments. Both men, not at least Haman, are flattered to be entertained by a Queen to whom mystery lends enchantment. At this banquet Esther requests that both the King and Haman accept her invitation to a next banquet.

Before this second banquet the King becomes aware that Mordechai has frustrated a plot to overthrow the government and he gives orders that Mordechai should be honored immediately. Of all people it is Haman who is commanded by the King to have Mordechai robed in royal apparel, driven on a handsome steed through the main streets of Shushan, and to proclaim for all to hear: "Thus shall it be done to a man whom the King deigns to honor."

Haman has hardly pocketed his pride after this unexpected turn of events when the second banquet in Esther's apartments takes place. At this banquet, Esther reveals her Jewishness and makes clear to the King that, should he allow Haman to execute his evil plans, the ultimate consequence is that the King will be left without her.

The tables are turned on Haman: it is he and his family who are to be exterminated. His power gets handed over to Mordechai. Salvation has come. The last chapters of the story record the crescendo of joy and feasting which follow the revenge taken upon those who had sought to exterminate the Jews. As a permanent reminder of the divine deliverance, Mordechai and Esther institute *Purim* as a national festival to be annually commemorated on the fourteenth day of *Adar*, the following day to be known as *Shushan Purim*.

The day of *Purim* is marked by the reading of the *Megillah Esther* (The book of Esther, which is generally known as *The Megillah*), joyous feasting, masquerading, play-acting and giving charity and gifts. *Megillah Esther* is chanted in the synagogue on the evening and morning of *Purim*. The reading of Haman's name from the *Megillah* is greeted by the children with the

*The day of **Purim** is marked by the reading of the **Megillah Esther** (The book of Esther, which is generally known as **The Megillah**), joyous feasting, masquerading, play-acting and giving charity and gifts.*

rattling of groggers (noisemakers) and the stamping of feet. A liturgical section (*Al Hanissim*) is introduced into the prayers and grace after meals on *Purim* reads as follows: "We thank Thee also for the miracles, for the redemption, for the mighty deeds and saving acts wrought by Thee, as well as for the wars which Thou has waged for our fathers in days of old, at this season." Then follows a short summary of the events commemorated.

Purim is a time "of sending portions to one another, and gifts to the poor" (Esther 9:22). *Shalach Manot* ("sending of gifts") to relatives and friends is a well-established *Purim* tradition in Jewish life. Gifts for the poor are traditionally provided by the contribution of *Mahtalt HaShekel* (half-shekel, considered the equivalent of a half-dollar) to recall the amount given by the Jews for the Temple in the month of *Adar*. It is a happy celebration, in which the consumption of alcohol is not only permitted but even promoted, "until one can no longer distinguish between the names Haman and Mordechai." A typical sweet eaten on this day is called *hamantashen*, or "Haman's pockets," filled triangular cookies.

Tisha B'Av

The blackest date in the Jewish calendar is, no doubt, the Ninth of Av. Not only have great disasters befallen the Jewish people on this date, but all subsequent calamities have also been a direct consequence of the destruction of the two Temples and of our subsequent exile from Eretz Israel.

The blackest date in the Jewish calendar is, no doubt, the Ninth of *Av*. Not only have great disasters befallen the Jewish people on this date, but all subsequent calamities have also been a direct consequence of the destruction of the two Temples and of our subsequent exile from *Eretz Israel*.

The *Mishnah* records the following five sad events that occurred on this day: "The decree that Israel should wander through the wilderness for forty years; the destruction of the First Temple by Nebuchadnezzar (in 586 B.C.E.), and of the Second Temple by Titus (in 70 C.E.); the fall of the fortress of Bethar; the subsequent fall of Bar Kochba and the massacre of his men; and the ploughing up of Jerusalem (by Hadrian in 135 C.E.)."

There are more sad events which occurred on the 9th of *Av*. On this day in 1290, King Edward I signed the Edict expelling his Jewish subjects from England; and, in Spain, in 1492, following the dreadful Inquisition, 300,000 Jews, led by Abarbanel, began to leave Spain, after Ferdinand and Isabella had signed the Decree for their expulsion. In most recent history, Hitler started the invasion of Poland on the 9th of *Av*, setting the earliest stages for the Holocaust. *Tisha B'Av* is the date of a host of sad memories, and there can be hardly a single member of the House of Israel who does not feel moved by the long list of tragedies experienced by our people associated with this day.

None of the misfortunes, however, have been so great or had such dreadful consequences as the destruction of our Sanctuary and the two thousand years of *Gallut*. Our sages, who foresaw it, ordered us to mourn this great calamity by abstaining from all food and work. The Talmud declares in the name of Rabban Gamliel that "if a man eats or drinks on the ninth of *Av*, it is the same as if he ate on *Yom Kippur* itself;" Rabbi Akiva said, "He who works on the ninth of *Av* will see no sign of blessing in it." The following Talmudic statement is probably the best explanation for our continued observance of *Tisha B'Av* in all its severity even today. Said the other sages, "He who eats and drinks on the ninth of *Av* will not live to see the rejoicing about Jerusalem, for the Scriptures say, 'Rejoice ye with Jerusalem, and be glad for joy with her, all ye that mourn for her'." This is to say, all who mourn the loss of her pristine greatness and glory, will witness the restoration of her ancient majesty. Yet the value of the Fast of *Av* lies not only in remembering the past and applying its lessons to the present, but also in recognizing the unity of our people, the continuity of our existence and the destiny which yet awaits fulfillment.

Other Holidays

In both the "At-a-Glance" reference at the end of this section and the Glossary you will find more information on other Jewish holidays. It is worth remembering that here we only give a brief and basic description of the holidays and that the interpretations of them, as well as the level of observance, vary considerably.

Yet the value of the Fast of Av lies not only in remembering the past and applying its lessons to the present, but also in recognizing the unity of our people, the continuity of our existence and the destiny which yet awaits fulfillment.

Holidays and the Calendar

Month (Num. days)	Holidays and Comments
Autumn — *Tishri* (30)	**1 *Rosh HaShanah:*** Occurs on the first and second of *Tishri*. *Rosh HaShanah*, the Jewish New Year, is designated as the day of judgment, a day of remembrance, a day of sounding the *Shofar*. It marks the start of the Ten Days of Penitence which conclude with *Yom Kippur*. With repentance and prayer we usher in the New Year and dedicate ourselves anew to the establishment, though righteous living, of God's Kingdom on earth. **3 Fast of Gedaliah:** Gedaliah was the only Jewish governor in the territory ruled by the Babylonians. He was assassinated by a Jew contracted by the rivals of the Israelites. Following this, the other loyal Jews fled to Egypt. The Babylonian king, Nabucodonosor, interpreted the fleeing as an admission of guilt and exiled the Jews of Babylonia, which marked the fall of the Kingdom of Judea. The murder of Gedaliah, therefore, meant the end of Jewish sovereignty. **10 *Yom Kippur:*** The Day of Atonement is a day of fasting and prayer, a day of confession of sin and supplication for forgiveness. **15 *Sukkot* (first day):** The Jewish festival of Thanksgiving, known also as the Feast of the Harvest Ingathering and the Season of Joy, expresses our gratitude to God for the bounties of nature. The *Sukkot* Festival reminds us of the period when our forefathers dwelt in these booths in their wanderings in the desert of Sinai. *Chol HaMoed*, the intermediate days of the holiday, are part of the festival week but are observed as half-holidays. **21 *Hoshanah Rabbah:*** The seventh day of *Sukkot*. Seven processions, with palm branches in hand, are made around the synagogue, and the verses of "*Hoshanah*" are chanted. **22 *Shemini Atzeret:*** "The Eighth Day of Assembly." Referred to in the Bible as "A Holy Convocation," it is celebrated in the concluding festival of the season. *Yizkor* (memorial services) is held. **23 *Simchat Torah:*** Celebrated on the second day of *Shemini Atzeret*, it is the holiday of rejoicing in the Torah. It celebrates the completion of the yearly reading cycle of the Torah and the beginning of the new cycle for the year. It underscores the idea that Torah study never ends: there is always something new to learn, new meanings, which in turn highlights the value Judaism gives to study. The end of Deuteronomy is read, immediately followed by the be-

Month (Num. days)	Holidays and Comments
Autumn — *Tishri* (30)	ginning of Genesis. During the ceremony in the synagogue, all the Torah scrolls are taken out of the *Aron Kodesh* and are carried throughout the Temple in a series of joyous processions full of dance and song. Those who read from the Torah are deemed "groom" and "bride," and the Torah, "*ketubah*." In that way, the idea of the pact is reaffirmed during this "anniversary." This is a synagogue-centered holiday.
Cheshvan (29 or 30)	
Winter — *Kislev* (29 or 30)	**25 *Chanukah*:** Beginning on the 25th of *Kislev* and ending on the second of *Teves*, *Chanukah*, the Feast of Dedication or the Feast of Light, commemorates the rededication of the Temple by the Maccabees in the year 165 B.C.E. The Maccabean triumph over the forces of the Syrian Greek King, Antiochus Epiphanes, was the first victory for a people's right to the freedom of worship. It is celebrated eight days, and lights are kindled.
Teves (29)	**10 Fast of *Asarah B'Teves*:** The fast of the Tenth of *Teves* marks the beginning of the siege of Jerusalem by the Babylonians in the year 586 B.C.E., which resulted in the destruction of the First Temple.
Shevat (30)	**15 *Tu B'Shevat*:** The fifteenth day of *Shevat*. The New Year for trees, the Jewish Arbor Day is observed in Israel, where school children plant trees. It also marks the beginning of Spring in Israel. It is customary to partake of the fruit of Israel on this day.
Adar (29; 30 on leap year)	**13 Fast of Esther:** This fast day marks the day when Queen Esther and the Jews of Persia fasted and prayed that God would save them from the destruction plotted by Haman. **14 *Purim*:** *Purim* celebrates the deliverance of the Jews of Persia from extermination through the help and intervention of Mordechai and Esther. It is customary to exchange gifts (*Shalach Monot*) with friends, and to distribute gifts to the poor. If there is a Jewish leap year, *Purim* is observed on the 14th day of Adar 2.
Spring — *Nisan* (30)	**15 First day of *Pesach*:** *Pesach*, known also as the season of freedom, is observed from the 15th to the 22nd day of *Nisan*. *Pesach* commemorates Israel's liberation from Egyptian bondage. During the days of the holiday, *matzot* are eaten in place of leaven bread. On the first and second nights of the festival the traditional *Seder* is held in the home. Passover also marks the early barley harvest in Israel. In memory of the ancient offering of an *Omer*, or measure of barely which our forefathers brought to the Temple on the second day of *Pesach*, and the counting of 49 days or 7 complete weeks

AT-A-GLANCE

Month (Num. days)		Holidays and Comments
Spring	*Nisan* (30)	until *Shavuot*, the ceremony of counting the *Omer* for 49 days begins with the night of the second *Seder*. *Chol HaMoed*, the four intermediate days between the first two days and last two days of *Pesach*, is a half-holiday during which the food restrictions of Passover are observed. **27 *Yom HaShoah*:** Day of remembrance of the horrors of the Holocaust (*Shoah*).
	Iyar (29)	**5 *Yom HaAtzma'ut*:** Israel Independence Day marks the rebirth of the New State of Israel. **18 *Lag B'Omer*:** The 33rd of the counting of the *Omer*. Weddings and other festivities which are forbidden during the other days of the *Omer* are permitted on this day because it marked the cessation of a plague which had caused the death of thousands of the followers of the great Rabbi Akiva, who rallied to the support of Bar Kochba in the last revolt against Rome (132-135 C.E.). *Lag B'Omer* is celebrated with outings, field games and festivities. **28 *Yom Yerushalayim*:** Jerusalem Day celebrates the reunification of the city on June 7, 1967, as a result of the Six Day War. Jerusalem is the most important city in Jewish tradition and history, mentioned more than 500 times in the Bible. It had been divided after the Independence War in 1948. When the section in Jordanian hands (which included the Western Wall) was taken in 1967, it was the first time in almost 2,000 years that the city was in Jewish hands. Due to its political connotations, this holiday is celebrated more in right-wing circles.
Summer	*Sivan* (30)	**6 *Shavuot* or *Shavuos*:** Observed on the 6th and 7th days of *Sivan*, *Shavuot*, known as the Feast of Weeks, completes exactly 7 weeks from the 2nd day of Passover, the counting of the *Omer*. *Shavuot* is also known as "The Season of the Giving of the Torah," for it was on *Shavuot* that the Torah was given to Israel at Mt. Sinai. The holiday is also referred to as the *Chag HaBikurim*, "The Festival of the First Ripe Fruit," since it marked the early wheat harvest and Jewish farmers brought their first ripe fruit to Temple as a thanksgiving offering. *Shavuo* is one of the three pilgrim festivals. Blintzes are typically eaten. The scroll of Ruth is read, since her story takes place during this time, but more importantly because she was a Jew by choice, a convert, a person who accepted the Torah. A tradition associated with this holiday is all-night study. It is during this holiday that we can appreciate the essential difference among contemporary Jewish movements, the difference from which all others seem to grow: Revelation, the way in which God reveals Himself to people, or the interaction between the I and the Other, the unifying force, the fusion of the binomial relationship present at all levels of existence (with exis-

Month (Num. days)	Holidays and Comments
Summer — *Sivan* (30)	tence itself as one of those terms). Was the Torah revealed by God at Sinai? Is it a compilation of different ways in which different people understood God at different times? Is God's Revelation static? Or is it a continual process? Does the Torah contain the word of God, or is it the word of God? Despite this fundamental difference, Judaism continues to be a religion because *all* Jews accept the Torah as a code, an instrument at the service of moral action.
Tamuz (29)	**17 The fast of *Shivah Asar B'Tamuz*:** This fast commemorates the first breach in the wall of Jerusalem during the siege in 586 B.C.E. This fast of the 17th of *Tamuz* marks the beginning of three weeks of mourning which ends with the 9th day of *Av*.
Av (30)	**9 *Tisha B'Av*:** This 9th day of the month of *Av*, or *Ab*, is a major fast day commemorating the destruction of the First Temple by the Babylonians in 586 B.C.E., and the Second Temple by the Romans in the year 70 C.E. Jews are required to fast 24 hours. The Book of Lamentations and other elegies are chanted at the synagogue services. The three weeks that precede *Tisha B' Av* are days of sadness when one must abstain from joyous celebration and weddings; if the 9th of *Av* Falls on the Sabbath, the fast is observed the following day.
Elul (29)	

Jews by Choice

Jewish Attitudes towards Conversion

Judaism has had a peculiar relationship towards its converts. In the beginning, it was one of the most proselytizing religions in the world. But after the 4th century C.E., due to religious persecution and conflicts with Christians, all missionary activity came to an end.

Another reason for the lack of interest in proselytizing lies at the core of the Jewish belief system. The Jewish people has never purported to have exclusive rights to a relationship with God. One need not be Jewish in order to be good or just, or to pray from the heart and be heard. Any man or woman, no matter what his or her beliefs, will have his or her reward if he or she acts righteously. Thus, there is no reason to "convert" non-Jews in order to "save their souls."

This lack of interest in proselytizing is reflected in rabbinical literature. There is only one small late, Talmudic tractate which addresses the practice and protocol of conversions, and it is only six pages long. Nonetheless, there have been conversions throughout all of Jewish history, for a great variety of reasons. Below are some basic Talmudic attitudes towards conversion:

1. Beloved are the converts to Judaism, for in many places in Scripture, God admonishes concerning them thus: "Do not vex nor oppress him" (Exodus 22:20); "You shall love the convert" (Deut. 10:19); "You must understand the feelings of the convert" (Exodus 23:9).

2. Beloved are the converts, for in many passages of Scripture God applies the same designation to them that He does to the born Israelite. Israelites are called servants of God... (Lev. 25:55), and converts are called servants of God... (Isaac 56:6), Israelites are referred to as friends of God... (Isaac 41:8), and converts are referred to as friends of God... (Deut. 10:18). Israelites are designated as belonging to the Covenant... (Gen. 17:13), and converts are designated as belonging to the Covenant... (Isaiah 56:6)

The Jewish people has never purported to have exclusive rights to a relationship with God. One need not be Jewish in order to be good or just, or to pray from the heart and be heard. Thus, there is no reason to "convert" non-Jews in order to "save their souls."

3. Beloved are converts. It was for their sake that our father Abraham was not circumcised until he was ninety-nine years old. If he had been circumcised at the age of twenty or thirty, one could not become a convert past that age. Therefore, God postponed it in Abraham's case until he reached the ninety-nine years of age, in order not to close the door to any future converts, and to give a premium reward according to one's age, increasing the reward of one who does His will...

4. When in these times, one seeks to become a convert to Judaism, we ask him, "Why have you seen fit to become a convert? Don't you know that in these times Jews are afflicted, pushed around, driven, and torn and that suffering descends upon them?" If he answers, "I know all this, and I am unworthy," we accept him at once, acquainting him with some of the lighter and some of the weightier commandments (...) making him aware of the penalties for violating the commandments (...) and of the rewards for observing them. (...) When he has been immersed and has come up from the ritual immersion, he is a Jew in every respect.

Accepting Judaism is not accepting only a religion; it means accepting a culture and becoming a part of a people, a people with a very tumultuous history.

Although there are traditional positions towards Jews by choice, attitudes towards conversion vary considerably. For instance, different rabbis expect different levels of Jewish knowledge. And some rabbis will refuse a future convert three times to make sure that he or she is absolutely sure that he or she wishes to convert. After all, accepting Judaism is not accepting only a religion; it means accepting a culture and becoming a part of a people, a people with a very tumultuous history. Maimonides wrote that all Jews, Jews by birth and Jews by choice, should pray to "our God, the God of our fathers." That is, Jews by choice fully assume all historical aspects of Judaism as well.

Regardless of how a possible convert is initially met, all are in agreement regarding to full acceptance of a Jew by choice. Once a person is Jewish, that person is always Jewish.

Regardless of how a possible convert is initially met, all are in agreement regarding to full acceptance of a Jew by choice. Once a person is Jewish, that person is always Jewish. The Talmud is clear on its insistence that Jews by choice are to be accepted as Jews in every regard, and traditionally rabbis have insisted that there should not be any distinction between Jews. For that reason there are those who do not take kindly to referring to a Jew by choice as such, since that person is a Jew, no more and no less. Moreover, Judaism not only accepts Jews by choice; many historical rabbis have praised converts, classifying them in an almost superior category. After all, the convert accepts Judaism willingly, by choice; without having to feel the threat of God lifting Mount Sinai over his or her head, saying, "Accept it or else..."

There is even a rabbinical homily that explains that the souls of all Jews were at Mount Sinai when Moses received the Torah and gave it to the Jewish people: the souls of the Jews still unborn, the souls of those who were going to convert to Judaism.

Upon reading the Bible, we encounter many Jews by choice. Abraham, Sarah, and Ruth are only three of them. Yet a case could be made that without them, Judaism might never have existed at all.

Becoming Part of the Covenant: The Formal Process

Each person's process is different. The time required depends on each case: it can last between one and several years. What is studied also varies, according to the knowledge of each person.

Each person's process is different. The time required depends on each case: it can last between one and several years. What is studied also varies, according to the knowledge of each person. Below are some of the generic steps:

1. Be accepted by a rabbi as a student. The candidate for conversion is called a *ger*, and the conversion process, *gerut*.

2. Study for a period of time determined by the rabbi. The kinds of courses could range from classes at the local synagogue in groups or privately, to classes at a yeshiva in Israel. Study often includes many different aspects: history, philosophy, theology, Hebrew language, literature, etc. However, it is not limited to a purely intellectual pursuit: Judaism is not ideas, but life. The *ger* should participate in holidays and in rituals, attend synagogue and become a part of the community, make his or her home a Jewish home: the community and the home are highly important spaces in Judaism. A famous rabbi once wrote, "Don't separate yourself from the community." Or as the Nobel prize winner, Elie Wiesel, similarly wrote, "Without community one cannot be Jewish." Judaism places a very high level of important on study (studying is considered a *mitzvah*), but there are other important aspects as well. We could even value such aspects as a sense of humor, food, etc. Many introduction to Judaism books, in their selection of recommended sources, include not only books on formal aspects of Judaism, but also Jewish films and songs.

3. Take a final exam which determines if one's knowledge of and attitude towards Judaism are adequate, and if the *ger* is absolutely sure he or she is ready and willing to take the last step, formal conversion to Judaism.

4. Appear before a *Beit Din*, or Rabbinical Court, made up of three knowledgeable Jews, at least one of whom is a rabbi. The convert will be questioned both about his or her Jewish knowledge as well as about the his or her motivation.

5. Circumcision is required by Conservative and Orthodox rabbis, while the Reform movement leaves it to the discretion of its rabbis. Consequently, a man who wants to convert Orthodox or Conservative has to undergo a *milah*, circumcision, or *atafat dam brit* (the drawing of a drop of blood symbolizing a ritual circumcision when the candidate is already circumcised).

6. Enter the *mikvah*, a ritual bath for ritual immersion. The candidate immerses him or herself three times while reciting blessings. Once the candidate emerges the last time, he or she is a Jew.

7. Sign a conversion certificate with one's chosen Hebrew name. Generally speaking, after the signing, the *ger* is formally introduced to the community in a religious ceremony, and he or she is handed the Torah.

8. The rabbi sends copies of the conversion certificate to a central agency, such as the American Jewish Archives in Cincinnati, OH, where it is archived. An additional copy is kept in the synagogue, while the *ger* keeps the original certificate.

9. Although no rabbi can or will ever help somebody to convert for financial gain, it is customary and appropriate to show one's appreciation for the rabbi's dedication and time by making a donation to a charity of the rabbi's choice.

The paths towards Judaism that, throughout history, thousands of men and women have voluntarily taken do not follow a model or pattern. The religious, emotional, and intellectual process that leads to a decision of this magnitude cannot be easily categorized.

Since Judaism is much more than a religion (it is a people and a way of life), the decision to become Jewish must be taken very seriously. There is a possibility that friends and family will not accept your decision. Moreover, there is a possibility that even your local Jewish community harbors prejudices towards converts, despite the fact that this violates Jewish laws, which clearly establishes the equality of all Jews. Once the formal process is over, the candidate is fully a Jew, with the same obligations and rights of a Jew by birth. One should even refrain from referring to him or herself as a "convert."

Becoming a part of a people has consequences that go beyond religion; there are also shared interests and a wide array of cultural practices. Therefore, one should also familiarize oneself with some of these ele-

Once the formal process is over, the candidate is fully a Jew, with the same obligations and rights of a Jew by birth. One should even refrain from referring to him or herself as a "convert."

ments, such as some Yiddish expressions, Jewish cooking or listening to Jewish comedians. Becoming a Jew means entering such a rich and diverse culture that one will always find Jewish topics of interest outside the direct realm of the religion.

Because of all of the aforementioned reasons, I suggest that a prospective convert think very seriously about his or her decision to become Jewish. This decision should be taken only if you absolutely believe in it and you are convinced that you could not feel happy or fulfilled any other way. It is normal for doubts and questions to arise. To resolve them, the best you can do is see a competent rabbi, one that inspires confidence, without fear. One must never forget that Judaism is not dogmatic. Doubt, questioning, debate, and reflection are not only not frowned upon, but highly valued in Jewish circles.

One must never forget that Judaism is not dogmatic. Doubt, questioning, debate, and reflection are not only not frowned upon, but highly valued in Jewish circles.

Converts and Israel

We have already discussed the differences among the different movements regarding conversion. It is worth mentioning that this topic, the so-called "Who is a Jew?" issue, is at the fore of the Jewish debate today. The identity of literally hundreds of thousands of Jews would be affected if, for instance, the Orthodox had the authority to impose their own definition. It is not limited to the *gerim*; it also affects the children and unborn children of mixed marriages.

As for the Israeli Law of Return, Jewish identity is not defined according to *Halacha*, despite the efforts of the ultra-Orthodox community, which is politically powerful in Israel. It is not probable that this will change in the near future, since it would drastically affect the relationship with the Jewish community in the U.S., which provides money and political influence to Israel.

Some years ago there was a very interesting case. It involved a Catholic priest of Jewish origin. According to *Halacha*, a Jew can never stop being a Jew. This priest attempted to immigrate to Israel under the Law of Return, but the Supreme Court declared that, upon converting to Catholicism, he was no longer Jewish. According to *Halacha*, the priest was Jewish, but a person born of a Jewish father or a *ger* converted by a non-Orthodox rabbi is not.

The spirit of the Law of Return was very clear in its day, in the years following the Holocaust: to protect anybody who could be considered a Jew. The Nazis considered a Jew anybody with at least one Jewish grandparent. Any Jew, converted by any rabbi of any movement in the Diaspora, can make *aliyah* under the Law of Return. It is also worth mentioning that this debate is not so much about the people whose Jewish identity is in question, as it is about the authority of non-Orthodox rabbis. The Orthodox do not recognize the authority of non-Orthodox rabbis and often they do not even recognize the authority of some Orthodox rabbis.

Any Jew, converted by any rabbi of any movement in the Diaspora, can make aliyah under the Law of Return.

Gerim and the Jewish Movements

	Orthodox	**Conservative**	**Reform**	**Reconstructionist**
Conversion Process	Requires instruction on Jewish life and an agreement to lead a Jewish life according to Orthodox rules (follow *Halacha*); requires *brit milah* and *tevilah* (ritual immersion in *mikvah*), as well as an Orthodox *Beit Din*	Requires instruction on Jewish life and an agreement to lead a Jewish life (*Halacha*); requires *brit milah* and *tevilah*, as well as a *Beit Din*	Requires instruction on Jewish life and an oral and written declaration of the free acceptance of Judaism and the intention to lead a Jewish life, recognizing the dangers of irrevocably belonging to the Jewish people; requires a *Beit Din*; *brit milah* and *tevilah* are not obligatory (in the U.S.) but are recommended	Requires *brit milah* and *tevilah*, as well as a *Beit Din*
Who is a Jew?	Any person born of a Jewish mother; Orthodox conversion	Any person born of a Jewish mother; conversion with *brit milah* and *tevilah*	Any person born of a Jewish mother or father if that person identifies with the Jewish people; conversion	Any person born of a Jewish mother or father if that person has received a Jewish education; conversion

Appendix

Where Judaism Differs

Differences between Judaism and Christianity

There are bookshelves filled with works on comparative religion. That is why this section will never be, nor does it intend to be, a comprehensive overview of the differences between Judaism and Christianity. The Christian faith is divided into many churches with very diverse beliefs, just as Judaism has branched out into major and minor denominations over the past 200 years. Comparing this diversity is a monumental task in itself. Furthermore, Judaism and Christianity are based on two incomparable paradigms. Where Christianity is based on a creed, Judaism is better defined by other parameters, such as a way of life. If one rejects the creed, one cannot be considered a Christian anymore, while one doesn't have to be religious and can still be through and through Jewish. Many of the early Zionist leaders sacrificed their lives to a Jewish ideal, yet they were far from religious.

Judaism and Christianity share a rich heritage, that of the Hebrew Bible (the "Old Testament," in Christian terminology), as well as a belief in one God, creator of the universe. They both share the Ten Commandments, the idea of a Covenant with God, the wisdom of the prophets, the brotherhood of all of humanity, the belief in peace and the hate of war, a democratic ideal in the political and social spheres, a belief in the undying nature of the human spirit, and finally, the belief that life has a meaning and a purpose.

These similarities, however, should not lead us to believe that Christianity is a continuation of Judaism. There are many differences, contradictions, and absolute disagreements in the very foundation of the Christian and Jewish identities. In the time of Jesus there were many different sects in Judaism. This diversity was the result of the brutality of Roman oppression, which led to such desperation that many tried to find their own explanation for this suffering and many were searching for signs of the coming of the Messiah. The situation for the Jews was so devastating that only the coming of the Messiah was seen as a possible solution. Christianity was born out of one of these Jewish sects, and therefore has inherited many Jewish aspects. But this birth was not the birth of a love child: Christianity broke with Judaism and created a new religion. Where the central belief of Christianity is that the acceptance of Jesus is necessary in order to be saved, the central belief of Judaism is that all religions are noble and that all people are God's children, be they Jews or Gentiles. Judaism does not believe that it is necessary for one to be Jewish in order to be saved; in fact, it believes that it is easier to be saved if one is *not* Jewish. In order to be saved, one must only lead an ethical life. This fundamental difference between Judaism and Christianity becomes most poignant in matters of conversion. For Christianity it is essential to proselytize in order to save as many people as possible, while for Judaism it is not essential to be Jewish in order to be saved, and thus Jews are reticent in seeking converts.

Below we will explore some religious aspects, which summarize the basic differences. The majority of these topics are dealt with in more details in other chapters of this book.

God

Judaism: God is one, indivisible, incorporeal, unique; an indivisible unity.
Christianity: A representation of the divinity of God the Father, God the Son, and the Holy Spirit (Trinity). Divinity is represented with and without a physical form.

The revolutionary contribution of Judaism more than four thousand years ago was monotheism. According to Judaism, God cannot be divided into parts and the Christian Trinity, therefore, is not accepted. God is one and unique. By extension, God is the creator of both good and evil, that which we like and that which we don't like. There is no evil force capable of equaling God's. For Judaism, the Trinity is a weakening of monotheism, and possibly a throwback to the pagan idea of many gods, which was so powerful in the days of the birth of Christianity. Moreover, in Judaism there is no defined concept of God. This fuels an ongoing debate and creates diverse opinions regarding the definition or idea of God. The only affirmation in

Judaism is that God is one. One can view, for instance, the search for a unitary explanation of the mysteries of life in thinkers of many different shades, such as Einstein, Buber, or Spinoza, as a typically Jewish impetus.

Jesus

Judaism: *Jesus was a human being, a Jew who taught the ideals of the Jewish faith. He was not the Messiah, the Christ, because no human being can be God and God cannot be human. Nor did he bring eternal peace: the Messiah will not have to "return" in order to bring it. The Messiah is only a human being sent by God and will bring peace and justice to the world. The Orthodox believe in a Messiah; Reform Jews believe in a Messianic Era, a time of truth, justice and peace on Earth. This will be brought about through our own ethical conduct.*

Christianity: *Jesus is the Messiah, the Christ, God who came to Earth as a human and sacrificed himself and was crucified, thereby saving humans from their sins. He returned to life and will come again, bringing the Heavenly Kingdom. The Messiah is God.*

The central belief of Christianity is that Jesus is the Son of God, part of the Trinity, and that only through him one can be saved. He is the revelation of God made flesh. He came to Earth to absorb the sins of all of humanity and to save those who accept his divinity.

The Jewish opinion of Jesus can vary. There are those who consider him an excellent storyteller, a great reformer, and a good human being. But no Jew can accept Jesus as the Son of God, but only as a human being. Jesus cannot save souls; only God can.

In Judaism, in order to obtain forgiveness for one's sins, one must search for it, mending whatever has been "broken." Sins committed against God are forgiven by asking God for forgiveness; sins committed against other human beings are forgiven by asking the injured party for forgiveness and by fixing whatever can be fixed, and by changing one's ways in order to avoid recurrence of the behavior that led to the "breaking." One must sincerely repent, in addition to fixing what has been broken. Prayer (which substituted animal sacrifice) is a part of repentance.

Jesus is not the Messiah. According to the Jewish point of view, the Messiah is a human being who will bring an eternal time of peace. We will know when the Messiah has arrived when the world is at peace and when justice prevails. This, clearly, did not happen when Jesus was on Earth, or after his death. Any human being can be the Messiah. Jews do not worry about finding out the identity of the Messiah since, as a human being, his presence will not affect our relationship with God: the personal relationship between each person and God is crucial.

The Christian idea that God will become human is considered a form of idolatry, which is strictly forbidden in Judaism. Observe the complete absence of "divine" images in Judaism, as well as the absence of any "cult of personality." Not even Moses enjoys the status enjoyed by the many saints, and non-saints, in Catholicism. During *Pesach*, we celebrate the Exodus from Egypt, where the presence of Moses is central. But Moses is barely mentioned in the *Haggadah*. Lastly, according to the Torah, the Messiah will lead all Jews to observe the laws of the Torah, and any person who attempts to change them is a false prophet. Jesus contradicted the Torah, he even declared that the *mitzvot* were no longer valid. For Christians, Jesus replaced Jewish law.

Free will and original sin

Judaism: Human beings have free will: we are responsible for our acts. Sins are negative acts that hurt others. People are born pure and they decide if they want to live ethically or not. Sin is an act that people can avoid and Jews have the responsibility to avoid it. Salvation is seen in communal terms, more than in individual ones. To obtain forgiveness, one asks for forgiveness and rectifies his or her actions and behavior. Nobody can achieve this for us. Judaism does not interpret the story of Adam and Eve as a reflection of the human fall from grace.

Christianity: *Sin is a condition of humanity. People are born in a state of original sin due to the disobedience of Adam. It is asserted that Christianity accepts the notion of free will, but each person must accept Jesus in order to be saved and he or she cannot avoid being born with original sin. Individuals cannot obtain forgiveness by themselves: they must believe in Jesus, who died for the sins of all of humankind.*

Judaism does not accept the idea of original sin, the idea that one is born "bad." Judaism believes that human beings are not born naturally good or bad. We have a good inclination and an evil inclination, but we have the free will to choose the path we desire. The price we pay for this freedom is the use that others make of their freedom, and that may potentially hurt us. It is not necessary to think too far in the past: the horrors of the Holocaust are still very close. Jewish ethics establishes the idea that human beings decide by themselves how they will act. That is due to the fact that the existence of temptation, and with it the possibility of sin, allows us to choose good and, as a result, gain moral merit. Judaism does not believe that human beings are at the will of a superior force, and therefore can choose to avoid moral error.

The Christian belief in original sin, the sin from which no human being can escape, obligates one to believe in a superior being that must save us. Hence, Jesus is the only viable path. For Christianity there are no other paths to salvation, only Jesus.

Death, Heaven, Hell

Judaism: *More attention is given to life on Earth, in this world. There are many opinions about the world to come; there is no formal eschatology. One need not be Jewish in order to be saved.*
Christianity: *One must accept Jesus in order to be saved. There is a clear dichotomy between life on Earth and the world to come. Christianity favors the subordination of life on Earth to its concept of the world to come.*

Judaism is a religion of life. The focus is on how to lead an ethical life on Earth, and to improve the world. The preoccupation with death and the world to come is postponed until the appropriate time. Judaism teaches that death is a natural occurrence, and it sees in death a way of giving meaning to life because, aware of our mortality, we are urged to make every moment on Earth count. Of course, worrying about death is natural: being frightened by death, the doubt about the fate of the soul after death, the ethical preoccupation with unjust death... all of these issues have their place in Jewish literature. However, there is no eschatology, a system of beliefs about death and the world to come. Very diverse attitudes coexist in the Jewish belief system, from the biblical idea to reincarnation, to nothingness.

It is worth repeating that Judaism does not believe that non-Jews will go to "Hell," and that the right to go to "Heaven" is reserved for Jews. Individual ethical behavior is the important and determining factor.

Body and Soul

Judaism: There is no hierarchy or dichotomy.
Christianity: As occurs with the dichotomy earthly life/eternal life, the soul is seen as distinct from the body and superior to it, as it is a reflection of the eternal.

Another fundamental difference is the idea of the body and the soul. Christianity places the two in a kind of conflict and considers the body to be inferior and potentially "dirty." Judaism, on the other hand, considers the body as something positive, a gift from God. This religious aspect gives way to a series of other differences between the two religions. The Christian focus is on the world to come, which is the home of the soul, and it reduces the importance of life on Earth, subordinating it to eternal life. Judaism focuses both on the life of the soul in the world to come and on the physical world, the "here and now." The body can be compared to the physical world, which can be "evil" for Christianity. Judaism has never assumed this feature; it gives no intrinsic value to one's removal from the physical world and the full exploration of it. Judaism focuses on the world that surrounds us, the "here and now." Judaism believes that God created the physical world so that we enjoy it and use it for our own self-fulfillment, not to make us miserable. Jewish spirituality is directly related to our effort to survive in this world in a way that uplifts us. Sex is not seen as something potentially negative and, as the Talmud states, if a person had the opportunity to try a new pleasure and rejects it, that person will have to explain his or her attitude in the world to come. Basically, Judaism does not remove itself from this world, but rather it attempts to elevate it. Compare this to Christian values, which made Mary a virgin, forced Catholic priests and nuns into celibacy, and had monasteries built in remote places

To summarize, Judaism is not worried about the idea each person has about God. Nor does it worry about each person's relationship with God, for it is a personal matter. Judaism focuses on our acts; there is no dichotomy between "law" and "faith." Christianity, on the other hand, focuses its attention on the belief of Christians.

The right to choose

Judaism: *Life begins at birth.*
Christianity: *Life begins at the moment of conception.*

As for abortion, Judaism does not share the attitude of the majority of Christian religions that life begins at conception. Nor is there an established position on the issue of abortion; there are different points of view among the movements, within each movement, and within each synagogue. Nevertheless, statistics reveal that the Jewish community is much more prone to defend the right of the mother to choose. Generally speaking, the fetus is seen as a human being when the head emerges during childbirth. However, abortion is tolerated in some circumstances. Even the most Orthodox rabbi will insist on an abortion if childbirth endangers the mother's life, since the abortion will save a life. Moreover, many Orthodox rabbis understand "danger" in both physical and psychological terms, so if having a child may negatively affect the mother's psychological well-being, an abortion may be justifiable. Despite the generalized consensus favoring the mother's right to choose, not even the most progressive rabbis trivialize the issue. Judaism has a pro-natality stance and abortion is seen as a last resort.

Suicide

Judaism: The act of suicide is so against our innate will to live that it must be the result of a psychological dysfunction.
Christianity: Committing suicide is a sin against the will of God, as God gives life.

Just as with most of the subjects discussed in this chapter, there is a wide array of views on the topic of suicide on both the Jewish and Christian side of the spectrum. However, where the general opinion within the main branches of Christianity affirm that suicide is a sin, the attitude of Judaism has shifted dramatically in recent history.

The traditional point of view in Judaism was the same as Christianity. As God gives us life, it is not for mortals to cast away that divine gift. Ending one's own life was considered such a grave sin that those who committed suicide could not be buried at the general grounds of a Jewish cemetery; there was a special section for those sinners, outside the fence.

Having a relative laid to rest in this special section caused great embarrassment to those who remained behind and that in itself violates one of the 613 *mitzvot*, which states that we have to avoid public embarrassment of others at all costs. While the discussion on which law should prevail lasted for centuries, a need for a decision on the issue became urgent in recent history. During the Holocaust many chose suicide over a slow and painful death. Were these people sinners? Should those who survived pass judgment over their decision?

Even before the Holocaust modern scientific and psychological insights made their entry into liberal Jewish thinking. The notion developed that we can't regard someone to be fully rational and in full possession of his or her mental capacities at the moment of the suicide. This originally liberal notion has slowly made its way into more traditional circles and, although there will still be local and individual differences of opinion, it becomes more and more accepted throughout the whole of Judaism that suicide is the unfortunate result of mental illness, and not a rationally deliberated sin against God.

Jewish Objects

Although the second of the Ten Commandments tells us not to worship any objects, the Jewish culture is rich with objects relating to Jewish religion. Judaism doesn't worship these objects, but uses them to worship and to fulfill the many commandments of the Torah. The often elaborate craftsmanship and use of precious materials that define these objects reflect the dedication to the fulfillment of the commandments, which is known as *Hidur Mitzvah* (Beautification of the Commandment). If we light candles on Shabbat, we should use the prettiest candleholders we can afford. If we use a different set of china at Passover, it ought to be our best china.

This principle has led to a wealth of ritual objects, which we find at the synagogue as well as in the home. It would be nearly impossible to give a complete overview of all ritual objects. The long history of Judaism, multiplied by the local customs and culture of individual communities, makes "Judaica" an expertise in itself.

To give a general insight, we have compiled an overview that touches on the synagogue and it's objects, on the holidays and festivals, and on the objects you can find in a Jewish home.

The Synagogue

As Jews settled outside Israel and lived too far away to fulfill their religious duties at the Temple in Jerusalem, an alternative for the Temple emerged: the synagogue, a place of gathering where prayers and Torah were read and where the sacrifices of the Temple were recalled.

The function of the synagogue as the center around which Jewish life evolved became even more poignant when in 70 C.E. Palestine and the Second Temple were destroyed by Rome and the Jews were scattered throughout the world. There was the need to preserve the unity of all the Jews in every corner of the world, to find a permanent substitute for the Temple and the Temple services. To answer these needs, synagogues were organized in every town where Jews lived. A common prayer book was developed in the language every Jew understood, no matter where he or she lived: Hebrew. In every community, the synagogue services became a substitute for the sacrifices of the Temple cult.

In its development to the present day the synagogue became more than a house of prayer, a religious center. It also became a house of study, a cultural center, as well as a house of assembly, a social center.

A house of prayer: Services are held daily, in the mornings and evenings, Sabbaths and holidays. Depending on the level of observance, Jews come regularly, if not daily to the synagogue for *Shacharit* (morning services), for *Mincha* (before evening services), and for *Ma'ariv* (evening services).

A house of study: From it's early days on, young people would spend many hours in the synagogue to study the Bible, commentaries on the Bible, and the Talmud. Adult Jews would also spend a few hours a week in the synagogue to study the Bible and the Talmud. The rabbi would lecture on the Talmud and matters of Jewish Law.

A house of assembly: The synagogue became a social center as all of Jewish life centered around it. Every event in life was celebrated in the synagogue: the birth of a baby, *Bar/Bat Mitzvah* ceremonies, weddings, and the commemoration of the deceased through reciting the *Kaddish*. Everyday problems were brought into the sphere of the synagogue since the rabbi was consulted on every aspect of life. Charities were collected in synagogues. A poor stranger would be taken care of in the synagogue. Law suits were announced, debts canceled and grievances for non-payment were called out.

Symbols and Religious Objects in the Synagogue

Ner Tamid, the perpetual light. In every synagogue you will find a perpetual light, placed either in a vessel containing oil and a wick or in an ornamental receptacle containing an electric bulb. It is usually suspended from the ceiling in front of the Holy Ark. The *Ner Tamid* had its origin in the early days of Israel's history. A perpetual lamp burned in the sanctuary in the wilderness, and also in the Temple at Jerusalem. The symbolism of the *Ner Tamid* was later transferred from the "Greater Temple" in

Jerusalem to the synagogues in all parts of the world. Lighting the *Ner Tamid* and placing the scrolls of the Torah Ark are the principal ceremonies in the dedication of a synagogue.

Menorah. The original *Menorah*, or seven-branched candelabrum, was made by Bezalel for the Tabernacle, and a duplicate of it was placed in the Temple at Jerusalem. Its counterpart is to be found in practically every synagogue. Its primary purpose was, and still is, to symbolize the light of the Torah. The *Menorah* has often been recognized as the symbol of universal Judaism.

Magen David, David's shield. This is the six-pointed star which is supposed to date back to the days of King David. It is also called Solomon's star. It has no religious significance and even its origin is vague, for it is not mentioned in the Bible or in the Talmud. However, it is universally displayed and is frequently considered the symbol of the Jewish people.

The Tablets of the Law. A reproduction of the two tablets of stone, containing the Ten Commandments, is seen in practically every synagogue. It is symbolic of God's Revelation on Mount Sinai.

Aron HaKodesh, the Holy Ark. This contains the scrolls of the Torah. It is a replica of the Ark of the Covenant which was erected in the Tabernacle to house the two tablets of the Ten Commandments and which was subsequently placed in the Holy of Holies in the Temple at Jerusalem. The ornamental drape of the Holy Ark is called *Parochet.*

Sefer Torah, the Holy Scroll. This contains the Pentateuch, or Torah, and it is the most sacred symbol of Judaism. It is written with indelible ink on parchment which is specially processed for that purpose from calves' skins. The writer, called *"Sofer,"* or "Scribe," is usually a pious man who devotes most of his life to this sacred work.

Keter Torah, a figurative crown of the Torah. This is usually designed on the *Parochet.* This is in keeping with a quotation from the Ethics of the Fathers (*Pirke Avot*)which lists the crown of the Torah with the crowns of the King and of the High Priest.

Bimah, the platform for the reading of the Torah. This pulpit, or reading desk, is usually decorated with the *Magen David* and covered with embroidered cloth.

Torah Ornaments. In addition to the ornate embroideries on its cloth mantle, or cover, the Torah is also adorned with many objects of art such as a crown, a breastplate, a pointer, and a pair of "*Etz Chayim*" (ornaments with bells).

Yad, which literally means "hand," is a pointer in the shape of a hand to assist with the reading of the Torah. Using a *Yad* prevents the grease and acid of our skin from reacting with the natural materials of the *Sefer Torah,* thus preventing it from deterioration.

The Lion of Judah. This is placed either on the Holy Ark or on the *Parochet.* It derives its origin from the time when Jacob, blessing his children before his death, compared Judah to a lion. The Jewish people, descendants of the tribe of Judah, have accepted the lion as their symbol.

Tallit, prayer shawl. Worn at daytime services and on the eve of *Yom Kippur,* this garment fulfils the commandment of wearing fringes on the corners of one's clothes to remember God's commandments. Although originally banned completely from Reform worship, it has slowly found its way back into the non-Orthodox branches of Judaism, where it is worn by both men and women, whereas in the traditional world the wearing of a *Tallit* is a strictly male privilege.

Tefilin, phylacteries. Black boxes with leather straps which are donned at daytime services, except for Shabbat and holidays. The boxes contain parchment scrolls with Torah verses, as it is written that one should wear the words of the Torah as a frontlet before ones eyes and as a sign upon one's hand.

Kippah, skull cap. The wearing of a skull cap as a sign of respect to a higher power has no clear origins, but for the fact that Judaism shares this custom with many other Middle Eastern and Semitic cultures. Its other name, *yarmulkah,* seems to derive from the Aramaic "*Yarmei Malkah,*" which means "Respect for the King."

Ritual Objects Related to Holidays and Festivals

Shabbat

Candleholders. Two candles are lit at the beginning of Shabbat, to remind us of God's words that we shall guard (*shamor*) and remember (*zachor*) the Shabbat.

Challa **cover.** As the two loaves of bread remind us of the double portion of manna we received in the desert on Friday, so the cover reminds us of the dew they were covered with.

Kiddush **Cup.** A goblet for wine of grape juice which is blessed first and then used to bless the Sabbath.

Havdalah **candle holder.** A holder for a braided candle used at the ceremony on Saturday night that separates the Sabbath from the ordinary weekdays.

Spice Box. At the *Havdalah* ceremony participants inhale the sweet fragrance of spices, to soften the gloom of the departing Sabbath.

ROSH HASHANAH AND YOM KIPPUR

As it is a custom to eat apples dipped in honey at *Rosh HaShanah* there are special apple and honey sets for this occasion. The **Shofar,** the ram or antilope horn, which is sounded on both of the High Holidays, is usually simple, yet can be decorated with precious metals. Specially shaped containers for the *Shofar* often show a high quality craftsmanship.

SUKKOT

The *lulav* and the **etrog,** two of the main symbols of the festival of *Sukkot,* are living materials and as such cannot be decorated. However, beautifully designed holders are available for both of them.

CHANUKAH

Chanukiah. Since the 9-armed candelabrum for *Chanukah* often has the same shape as the 7-armed *Menorah,* the *Chanukiah* is often called by the name of the latter, although technically this is incorrect.

Dreidel. Although the spinner known as the *dreidel* has become a fun object for innocent gambling to win *Gelt* (chocolate coins), its origins are educational. When the Syrians occupied Judea, Jewish children were forbidden to study the Torah. However, this edict was defied by pretending to play the *dreidel* game when Syrian soldiers passed by. The four symbols on the *dreidel* (*nun, gimel, hey* and *shin*) announce, "A great miracle happened there," so even this simple toy reminds the children of the reason for *Chanukah.* In Israel, the symbols are changed to say "A great miracle happened *here*" (*nun, gimel, hey* and *peh*). There is another meaning to the letters on the *dreidel.* In mystical *Kabbala* teachings, each stands for one of the four empires that have tried to destroy the Jewish people: Babylonian, Persian, Greek, and Roman.

PURIM

Although *Purim* is known for its costumes and its theatrical plays, it knows only one ritual object, the **grogger** (noise-maker). At *Purim* the community gathers in the synagogue to hear the reading of the *Megillah Esther*, the Esther Scroll. Every time the name of Haman is mentioned, the community expresses its discontent by making as much noise as possible, using the groggers.

PESACH

As the holiday of Passover knows many strict dietary laws to avoid the presence of *chametz*, leaven, it is customary to have a separate set of kitchen utensils and china to be used only during the days of Passover. The ritual objects relating to *Pesach* are used at the *Seder* dinner, when the story of the liberation from Egypt is recounted.

Seder **plate.** The *Seder* plate has sections for the traditional foods that symbolize the various aspects of the *Pesach* story: the shank bone, the roasted egg, lettuce, parsley, *charoset,* and bitter herbs.

Matzah **plate.** A separate plate for the *Matzah.*

Matzah **cover.** A cloth cover for the *Matzah*, sometimes double-functioning as the cover for the *Afikoman* when it is hidden, although there are separate *Afikoman* bags for this purpose.

Elijah's **cup:** As it is believed that the prophet Elijah will come down from heaven to announce the coming of the Messiah, the doors are opened at the *Seder* meal and a special cup for Elijah is filled with wine, in the hope that he might come as a forbearer of the world to come.

The other Jewish holidays don't have any specific ritual objects, although one might find an ***Omer* calendar** in traditional synagogues and homes. The *Omer* is the seven week period between *Pesach* and *Shavuot* and its days have to be counted in the daily prayers. The calendar makes sure this is done correctly.

Symbols and Ritual Objects at Home

A Jewish home is often recognizable by the ritual objects as mentioned before, like the *Seder* plate on display or the candelabrum used for *Chanukah*. Other objects that distinguish a Jewish home are:

Mezuzah. To be precise, *Mezuzah* is the Hebrew word for "door post," but it usually refers to a small tube or case, made of wood or metal, containing a rolled piece of parchment with two passages from the Book of Deuteronomy. Through a small opening in the upper part of the *Mezuzah* one sees the Hebrew word "*Shaddai*" ("God"). The *Mezuzah* is fixed in a slanting position to the upper part of the door post at the right side as one enters the home. When the *Mezuzah* is placed on the door post, one recites the blessing: "Blessed be Thou, Lord Our God, King of the Universe, who has commanded us to affix the *Mezuzah*."

The purpose of the *Mezuzah* is to fulfill the biblical command: "Thou shalt write them on the door posts of thy house and upon thy gates." Another reason given by Maimonides is that "the *Mezuzah* reminds man, when entering or leaving, of the unity of God and of the duty to love Him and to keep His commandments." It also means that God's blessings and protection are bestowed upon a house where there is a *Mezuzah*. The *Mezuzah* is also a sign that in such a home lives a believer in God and in the teachings of the Jewish faith.

Books. Books are considered to be a most precious possession in Judaism. Depending on the level of observance and involvement, one will find a prayer book, a Bible, a *Haggadah* and books on various Jewish topics in Jewish homes.

Mizrach. Jews are supposed to face Jerusalem when praying. When a synagogue is erected, the architecture guarantees that when one faces the Holy Ark, one is facing Jerusalem. When one prays at home, a *Mizrach* (lit. "East"), a plaque mounted to the eastern wall, provides the proper direction.

Ketubah. The *Ketubah* (marriage contract) is the usually beautifully decorated and illuminated marriage contract and is regarded as the proud symbol of the desire to create a Jewish family. Therefore it can often be found on one of the walls in a Jewish home.

Tzeddakah **box.** As giving to those less fortunate is not an option, but an obligation, a box for charity has a prominent place in the home.

Depending on the involvement of the family, one can find art with Jewish subjects or by Jewish artists, a plaque with a blessing for the home for instance. Depending on the level of observance and the financial circumstances of the family, there can also be architectural elements typical of Judaism. When possible, an observant family will have a kitchen tailored to the laws of *kashrut*, with separated counters and sinks. In the more established communities, where Jews have been able to build their own houses and the climate isn't very favorable to the celebration of *Sukkot*, one can even find sun rooms with retractable roofs.

Blessings and Prayers

Judaism has a very special way to bring the divine into daily life by means of *brachot* (single: *bracha*), blessings. Originally, a blessing was said when one performed or complied with one of the 613 *mitzvot* of the Torah, thus acknowledging one's loyalty and faithfulness to the word of God. Over history, the rabbis recognized that it is human nature to lose a certain sensitivity towards the miracle of nature and take for granted what seems to be common, like waking up in good health. Therefore, the blessings were extended beyond the laws of the Bible and their function expanded to both acknowledgement of God's will and thanksgiving for God's presence. There are blessings for seeing lightning, for traveling, for experiencing the ocean for the first time, for creating diversity among people, etc.

The *brachot* have an common formula and all start with *Baruch Atah Adonai, Eloheinu Melech Ha'Olam...* ("Blessed are You, Eternal our God, Ruler of the Universe..."). When it is a blessing for thanksgiving, that which is thanked for follows directly after this formula. When it concerns a blessing relating to the laws of the Bible, the formula is *Baruch Atah Adonai, Eloheinu Melech Ha'Olam, asher kideshanu bemitzvotav, vetzivanu...* ("Blessed are You, Eternal our God, Ruler of the Universe, Who sanctified us by His commandments, and has commanded us..."), followed by the commandment.

The *Sh'ma*

The *Sh'ma* is the central creed of the Jewish faith, expressing God's unity and sovereignty. The *Sh'ma* is to be recited twice a day: when waking up and when going to sleep.

Sh'ma Yisrael, Adonai Eloheinu, Adonai Echad.
Hear Israel, the Eternal is our God, the Eternal is One.
Baruch shem k'vod malchuto l'olam va'ed.
Blessed is God's glorious Ruling forever and ever.

Brachot for Shabbat

The candles

Usually performed by women, but may be done by men as well, the blessing is recited after the candles are lit.

Baruch Atah Adonai, Eloheinu Melech Ha'Olam, asher kideshanu bemitzvotav, vetzivanu lehadlik neer shel Shabbat.

Blessed are You, Eternal our God, Ruler of the Universe, Who sanctified us by Your commandments, and has commanded us to kindle the lights of Shabbat.

Kiddush

Kiddush literally means "sanctification" and is meant to separate Shabbat from the common weekdays. Traditionally, the *Kiddush* is sung by the father on Friday night after the mother has kindled the Shabbat candles.

In an undertone:
Va'yehi erev, va'yehi voker yom ha'shishi.

Aloud:
Va'yechulu ha'shamayim ve'ha'aretz v'chol tzeva'am. Va'yechal Elohim ba'yom ha'shevi'i melachto asher asa, va'yishbot ba'yom ha'shevi'i mikol melachto asher asa. Va'yevarech Elohim et yom ha'shevi'i va'yekadesh oto, ki vo shavat mikol melachto asher bara Elohim la'asot.

Baruch Atah Adonai, Eloheinu Melech Ha'Olam, borei peri ha'gafen.

Baruch Atah Adonai, Eloheinu Melech Ha'Olam, asher kideshanu b'mitzvotav v'ratzah vanu, v'Shabbat kodsho b'ahavah u'v'ratzon hinchilanu, zikaron lema'aseh beresheet. Ki hu yom techilah le'mikraei kodesh, zeicher li'yetziat Mitzrayim; Ki vanu vacharta v'otanu kidashta mi'kol ha'amim, veShabbat kodshecha be'ahavah u'veratzon hinchaltanu. Baruch Atah Adonai Mekadesh HaShabbat.

And it was evening, and it was morning of the sixth day, the creation of heaven and earth were completed with all of their array. On the seventh day God completed all of God's creation and rested on the seventh day from the creative activity which God had done. God blessed the seventh day and made it holy, for on it God rested from all the work which God had done.

Blessed are You, Eternal our God, Ruler of the Universe, Who sanctified us with Your commandments and desired us, and gave us His holy Sabbath with love and pleasure, as an inheritance, a remembrance of the act of creation. For the Sabbath is the first of the holidays, a remembrance of the Exodus from Egypt. For You have chosen us, and made us holy from all the nations, and You gave us Your holy Sabbath with love and pleasure; Blessed are You, Holy Ruler, who sanctifies the Sabbath.

The Bread
The loaves of bread are held together and, after reciting the blessing, pieces are handed out to everyone present at the dinner table.

Baruch Atah Adonai, Eloheinu Melech Ha'Olam, hamotzi lechem min ha'aretz.
Blessed are You, Eternal our God, Ruler of the Universe, Who brings forth bread from the earth.

Blessing over the children
After the blessing over the bread, place your hands on your children and recite the appropriate blessing.

For boys:
Y'simcha Elohim k'Efrayim v'chi'M'nasheh.
May God make you like Ephraim and Menasseh.

For girls:
Y'simcha Elohim k'Sarah, Rivkah, Rachel v'Lei'ah.
May God make you like Sarah, Rebecca, Rachel, and Leah.

For both:

Y'varech'cha adonai v'yishm'recha.
May God bless you and keep you

Ya'eir adonai panav eilecha vihuneka.
May God's presence shine upon you and grant you graciousness.

Yisa Adonai panav eilecha v'yaseim l'cha shalom.
May God's presence be with you and grant you peace

Havdalah

Just as the beginning of Shabbat is marked by the candles and the *Kiddush*, the end of Shabbat is celebrated with a short ceremony called *Havdalah*, which means "separation," to distinguish the Shabbat from the ordinary weekdays ahead of us. You will need three things for this ritual: a glass of wine, some fragrant spices, and a special *Havdalah* candle.

Blessing over the wine

Baruch Atah Adonai, Eloheinu Melech Ha'Olam, borei peri ha'gafen.
Blessed are You, Eternal our God, Ruler of the Universe, Who created the fruit of the vine.

The second blessing is recited over fragrant spices. The spices represent a compensation for the loss of the special Shabbat spirit. The spices commonly used are cloves, cinnamon, or bay leaves. They are commonly kept in a special decorated holder called a *b'samim* box, which is passed around so everybody can smell the scent of the spices.

Baruch Atah Adonai, Eloheinu Melech Ha'Olam, borei minei b'samim.
Blessed are You, Eternal our God, Ruler of the Universe, Who creates varieties of spices.

The third blessing is recited over the special, multiwicked *Havdalah* candle.
Baruch Atah Adonai, Eloheinu Melech Ha'Olam, borei m'orei ha'eish.
Blessed are You, Eternal our God, Ruler of the Universe, Who creates the light of the fire.

The final blessing is the *Havdalah* blessing itself, the blessing over the separation. The blessing is recited over the wine. After the blessing is complete, the wine is drunk. A few drops of wine are used to extinguish the flame from the candle.

Baruch Atah Adonai, Eloheinu Melech Ha'Olam, hamavdil bayn kodesh l'chol,
Blessed are You, Eternal our God, Ruler of the Universe, Who distinguishes between the sacred and the secular,

bayn or l'choshech, bayn Yisrael la'amim,
bayn yom hash'vi'i l'shayshet y'may hama'aseh.
between light and dark, between Israel and the nations,
between the seventh day and the six days of labor.

Baruch Atah Adonai, hamavdil bayn kodesh l'chol.
Blessed are You, Eternal our God, who distinguishes between the sacred and the secular.

Chanukah

Of all Jewish holidays, *Chanukah* is probably the most popular and most celebrated, appealing to every level of observance with its universal messages of freedom of religion and the spark of hope that illuminates even the darkest of times.

Baruch Atah Adonai, Eloheinu Melech Ha'Olam, asher kideshanu bemitzvotav, vetzivanu lehadlik neer shel Chanukah.

Blessed are You, Eternal our God, Ruler of the Universe, Who sanctified us by his commandments, and has commanded us to kindle the lights of *Chanukah*.

Baruch Atah Adonai, Eloheinu Melech Ha'Olam, she'asa nisim la'avotenu ba'yamim hahem bazeman hazeh.

Blessed are You, Eternal our God, Ruler of the Universe, Who wrought miracles for our fathers in days of old, at this season.

The following blessing, known as the *Shehecheyanu*, is said on the first night only. It is Judaism's "all purpose" blessing and can be said any time when one feels to have reached a special moment in life.

Baruch Atah Adonai, Eloheinu Melech Ha'Olam, shehecheyanu, vekiyemanu, vehigiyanu lazeman hazeh.

Blessed are You, Eternal our God, Ruler of the Universe, Who has kept us alive, and has preserved us, and enabled us to reach this season.

The *Mezuzah*

Beginning to lead a Jewish life literally starts at your front door with the affixing of a *mezuzah*, proclaiming to the world that your house is a Jewish home and that those who live there are mindful of the Torah and its *mitzvot*.

Baruch Atah Adonai, Eloheinu Melech Ha'Olam, asher kideshanu bemitzvotav, vetzivanu likbo'a mezuzah.

Blessed are You, Eternal our God, Ruler of the Universe, Who sanctified us by his commandments, and has commanded us to affix a *mezuzah*.

After that one recites the *Shehecheyanu*.

The *Kaddish*

This prayer is another example of Judaism's rich history. The *Kaddish* is not written in Hebrew, but Aramaic. Only the last strophe is in Hebrew.

The *Kaddish*, although a prayer for the mourners, doesn't mention death once. We recite it to remind us that God is there in the most incomprehensible moments of sorrow and it allows us to express our gratitude to God for giving us the ability to love and to remember.

Yitgadal v'yitkadash sh'mei raba,
b'alma div'ra chirutei, v'yamlich malchutei
b'chaiyeichon uv'yomeichon
uv'chaiyei d'cholbeit Yisrael,
ba'agala uvizman kariv,
v'im'ru: Amein.

Y'hei sh'mei raba m'varach
l'alam ul'almei almaya.

Yitbarach v'yishtabach,
v'yitpaar v'yitromam v'yitnasei,
v'yithadar v'yitaleh v'yithalal, sh'mei d'kud'sha, b'rich hu,
l'eila min kol birchata v'shirata,
tushb'chata v'nechemata, daamiran b'alma,
v'im'ru: Amein.

Y'hei sh'lama raba min sh'maya,
v'chayim, aleinu v'al kol Yisrael,
v'im'ru: Amein.

Oseh shalom bimromav,
hu yaaseh shalom aleinu v'al kol Yisrael,
v'im'ru: Amein.

May the great Name of God be exalted and sanctified, throughout the world, which he has created according to his will.

May God's dominion be established in your lifetime and in your days, and in the lifetime of the entire household of Israel, swiftly and in the near future; and say: Amen.

May God's great Name be blessed, forever and ever.

Blessed, praised, glorified, exalted, extolled, honored elevated and lauded be the Name of the holy one, blessed is God, above and beyond any blessings and hymns, praises and consolations which are uttered in the world; and say: Amen.

May there be abundant peace from Heaven, and life, upon us and upon all Israel; and say: Amen. May God, Who makes peace in his high holy places, bring peace upon us, and upon all Israel and upon all the world; and say: Amen.

Glossary

A

Adonai "Our Lord," one of the names of God.

Aggadah The non-halachic texts of the Talmud and *Midrash*, such as folklore, legends, theological texts, biographies, etc.

Afikoman A Greek word which means "dessert." At the time of the Temple, the meal finished with lamb. Today we use *matzot* (sing. *matzah*) as the dessert of the Passover *Seder*. To keep children's attention, we hide the *afikoman* at the beginning of the *Seder*. The children try to find it, and they "steal" it when the adults "aren't looking." We must eat the *afikoman* in order to conclude the *Seder*, and therefore the adults have to pay a "ransom" to the children for them to release the *afikoman* they hold "hostage."

Alef-Bet The Hebrew alphabet.

Aleinu The last prayer of any service, which underscores the sovereignty of God.

Aliyah "To go up." It is used when a Jew "goes up" to recite the blessing before and after the Torah reading, or when a Jew emigrates to Israel.

Al Chet The prayer of repentance recited by the entire congregation in the third person plural on *Yom Kippur*. It contains a list of sins for which we ask for forgiveness.

Am Israel The People of Israel or the Jewish People (the descendents of Jacob, also known as "Israel").

Amidah A silent prayer recited standing. It contains 18 blessings. It is also known as *Sh'mone Esre* ("18 Blessings").

Amoraim "Speakers." It refers to the rabbinic teachers who produced the *Gemara* in the 3rd and 4th centuries C.E.

Aninut The time between death and burial. During this period the mourners are legally exempt from their religious obligations since they must attend to the needs of the deceased, and because "he who is busy with the fulfillment of a *mitzvah* is exempt from the fulfillment of another."

Arbah Minim The four branches and fruits used during *Sukkot*. See also *Lulav* and *Etrog*.

Aron Kodesh "Holy ark." The ark that contains the Torah scrolls.

Arvit Evening service, also known as *Ma'ariv*.

Aseret Y'may Teshuvah "The Ten Days of Repentance." The period from *Rosh HaShanah* to *Yom Kippur* is a 10-day period and the entire period is considered a time for introspection and repentance. This 10-day period is also known as *"Yamim Nora'im,"* the Days of Awe.

Ashkenazim Term used to refer to Jews from Central and Eastern Europe who generally follow the medieval Jewish customs of German Jewry. They comprise the largest Jewish community.

B

B.C.E. "Before the Common (or Christian) Era," used instead of "B.C."

Bamidbar The Book of Numbers.

Bar Aramaic for "son."

Bar Mitzvah "Son of the commandment." It refers to the 13-year-old boy as well as to the ceremony. This ceremony marks the religious coming of age of the boy. The boy accepts the obligation to obey the commandments and to lead a Jewish life. Although a boy is considered a *Bar Mitzvah* automatically by reaching the age of 13, there normally is an elaborate ceremony. This ceremony demands years of study and a general preparation (basic Hebrew, Jewish studies, etc.). The origins of the ceremony are not biblical or Talmudic, but rather date from the Middle Ages. During the ceremony, the *Bar Mitzvah* leads a part of the service, reads a portion of the Talmud, a *Haftorah,* and the blessings before and after the Torah readings. He usually gives a short speech to the congregation. In some communities, it is the first time he will wear a *Tallit.*

Bat Aramaic for "daughter."

Bat Mitzvah "Daughter of the commandment." It refers to the 12-year-old girl as well as the ceremony. See *"Bar Mitzvah"* above.

Beit Din A rabbinic court comprised of three rabbis who resolve legal disputes and determine if a possible convert is prepared.

Beit Knesset "House of gathering." A synagogue. The word "temple" is also used, as is the Yiddish word, *"Shul."*

Ben Hebrew for "son."

Beresheet The Book of Genesis.

Bimah The "pulpit" in a synagogue.

Blintze Crêpe with cheese or fruit; eaten on *Shavuot.*

Bracha A blessing; any prayer beginning with: *"Baruch atah..."*

Brit A "covenant." It refers to the covenant between God and the Jewish People.

Brit Habbat The ceremony in which a newborn is given a Hebrew name.

Brit Milah The "covenant of circumcision." It refers to the circumcision of an 8-day-old boy or a male convert. Normally, the term *"bris"* is used, which comes from Ashkenazi Hebrew. Birth is the first part of the life cycle. The *bris* is a symbol of the covenant between Abraham and God. Genesis contains the passage in which God commands Abraham and his descendants to circumcise themselves as a sign of their loyalty to this covenant. Traditionally, a *mohel* performs the circumcision and a rabbi performs the ceremony. Surgeons can learn how to become *mohalim*.

C

C.E. "Common (or Christian) Era." These initials are used instead of "A.D." because the latter implies that Jesus is the son of God, a concept rejected by Judaism and Islam, among other religions.

Chag Sameach The greeting used during the holidays, meaning "happy holiday." In Yiddish, the equivalent is *"Gut Yuntif."*

Chai "Life." It is used very frequently, underscoring the high value Judaism places on life. It is used in jewelry and other ornaments. When one gives to charity, he or she usually does so in multiples of 18, the numerical value of the word. A typical toast is *"L'chaim"* ("to life").

Challah Special egg bread served on the Sabbath and other holidays. It is usually sweet (sometimes with raisins), yellowish, and covered with sesame seeds. The *challah* eaten on *Rosh HaShanah* is round and has raisins (to symbolize the yearly cycle and the hope for a sweet New Year). In some homes, two *challot* are made or bought, to remember the double ration of manna that, according to the Bible, God gave the Israelites in the desert after the Exodus. God took care of the daily needs of the Israelites, providing them with two portions of manna of Friday so they could refrain from collecting food on the Sabbath.

Chametz Fermented bread or any product made of wheat, rye, etc. It refers to the substances that are prohibited during *Pesach*.

Chanukah 8-day holiday that commemorates the rededication of the Temple of Jerusalem after a struggle for religious freedom, around the year 164 B.C.E.

Chanukat HaBayit The brief ceremony in which a *Mezuzah* is affixed to the door; it refers to the dedication of the house.

Chanukiah The 8-arm candelabrum, with an extra (normally separated) arm for the *Shamash*, which lights the 8 candles. Used during *Chanukah*.

Charoset One of the foods present in the Passover *Seder*, used to remind us of the tasks Jews in Egypt engaged in when they were slaves.

Chassidim Pl. of *chassid*. It can refer simply to pious people, according to its literal meaning. It sometimes refers to those who resisted the anti-Jewish policies which would ultimately lead to the rebellion celebrated during *Chanukah* in the 2nd century B.C.E., or to the mystics of the 13th century, or to the followers of the Chassidic (or Hassidic) movement founded in the 18th century by Rabbi Israel Baal Shem Tov.

Chavurah An informal group that meets to study, worship, and celebrate. It is normally egalitarian and does not have a rabbi.

Chavurah kaddishah An organization that prepares the dead for burial.

Chazan A cantor.

Cheder "Room." It refers to the Jewish school (in a room) typical of the
small villages of Central Europe in the 19th and 20th centuries. The
word was still used in the US in the beginning of the 20th century in
Jewish immigrant communities to refer to Hebrew school.

Chuppah A structure covered by a cloth and flowers under which a couple
gets married. It symbolizes the home where they will live.

Confirmation A ritual of Reform Judaism that originally replaced the *Bar
Mitzvah* ceremony. But with time, once the *Bar Mitzvah* ceremony was
reincorporated, Confirmation also remained. It is celebrated on *Shavuot*
and the participants reaffirm that they choose to remain loyal to the
Jewish People. *Shavuot* commemorates the acceptance of the Torah. The
Jews had been liberated from Egypt but they became truly free when
they accepted the Torah. Confirmation represents the free acceptance
of Judaism. This ceremony highlights the mutually inclusive idea of
Jews as a Chosen People and as a Choosing People; it reaffirms the
idea that all Jews are Jews by choice, reflected in the acceptance of
God's covenant by Abraham and Sarah.

D

Daven Yiddish for "to pray." It is often confused with the swaying movement of the body used by traditional Jews when they pray.

Devarim The Book of Deuteronomy.

Diaspora The dispersion of Jews throughout the world after the fall of the
Second Temple in 70 C.E. Although Judaism has always been the religion of a wandering people (remember Abraham), the Diaspora as
such did not exist until after the Jews setteled in the Promised Land
and then were forced to leave. This began after the destruction of the
First Temple, but was accelerated and made definitive with the destruction of the Second Temple. Today, there is considerable debate
about the nature of the Diaspora due to different ideas regarding the

State of Israel. Outgrowths of the Diaspora are the rabbinic tradition, the synagogue, and the Talmud (which provided a framework for Jews living dispersed throughout the world).

Dreidel A Yiddish word referring to the typical *Chanukah* game. In Hebrew, it is called a *"sevivon."*

E

El Molei Rachamim A prayer for the deceased.

Elohim, El Hebrew words referring to God.

Emancipation The events of the 19th century which permitted Jews to receive full civil rights in European society.

Eretz Yisrael Or *Israel.* "The land of Israel."

Erev "Eve." It is used to refer to the eve of a holiday.

Etrog A citrus fruit used during *Sukkot.*

F

Fleishig Yiddish for "meat." It is used to describe the *Kosher* foods that contain meat and, therefore, cannot be eaten with dairy products.

G

Gabbai A lay person who, during the Torah reading, helps the service leader. He or she is called to the *Bimah* for an *Aliyah.*

Gallut "Exile." It refers to both the several expulsions from Israel and, later, the lack of a homeland, the fact that Jews are always "strangers." Therefore, it refers to living in the Diaspora and to a state of physical and spiritual alienation.

Gan Eden The Garden of Eden; Paradise.

Gaon A title given to a Jewish leader of the Babylonian academy and, later, to noteworthy talmudic scholars. Pl. *geonim*.

Gefilte Fish A mix of fish and spices served cold with horseradish.

Gehinom "The Hinom Valley." A transitory place of punishment after death, according to ancient Jewish tradition.

Gelt Yiddish for "money." It refers to a gift given to children during *Chanukah*.

Gemara It generally refers to the entire Talmud, discussions about *Mishna*, and the decisions made during those discussions. In a more limited sense, it refers to the text pertaining to the *Amoraim* generation, which "completed" the *Mishna* and produced the Talmud.

Gematria An interpretative resource invented during the time of rabbinic Judaism. It deals with the numerical value of words.

Get Document of divorce.

Goy Hebrew word which refers to a person or a nation. The most widely used meaning comes from Yiddish and refers to a Gentile.

H

Hadassah Women's Zionist organization in the US.

Haftorah Section of biblical prophets read in the synagogue immediately after the Torah portion.

Haggadah "Story." The *Haggadah* read during the *Seder* contains the story of the miserable life of the Hebrews in Egypt and how they were liberated from slavery. It also contains many beautiful prayers and hymns.

Halacha Any normative code: laws, customs, rituals, etc., established by rabbinical jurists; that is, prescriptions for the practical application of *mitzvot*. If something it halachic, it is considered normative conduct. Some Jewish movements consider these prescriptions obligatory, while others do not. Any non-halachic text in the Talmud or *Midrash* is called *Aggadah* (folklore, legends, theology, etc.).

Hallel Psalms 113-118, recited at the end of morning services on holidays.

Hamantashen Yiddish for "Haman's pockets." They are triangular cookies filled with fruit and served on *Purim*.

HaShem "The Name." It refers to God.

Haskalah The Jewish rationalist Enlightenment which began in Europe in the 18th century.

Havdalah "Separation." The ceremony that concludes the Sabbath and which includes wine, spices, and candles. Smelling the spices symbolizes hope for a fragrant week, and the light of the candles symbolizes hope for a "brilliant" and happy week. At the end, the candle is put out with the wine and we are left in darkness. But this darkness is not the lack of hope, but rather a reminder of the conclusion of the Sabbath and the return to the "real world," which is itself in darkness and is in need of repair. The ceremony is a joyous way of finding energy to begin the week and participate in it as well and as fully as we can.

I

Israel The name given to the patriarch Jacob by God. In biblical times, the name referred to the northern tribes, but also to the entire nation. Today, it also refers to the State of Israel.

K

Kabbala A Jewish mystical system.

Kabbalat Shabbat "Welcoming the Sabbath." It is the first part of the service held on Friday night, and is often used to refer to the entire service.

Kaddish One of the most sacred prayers, sanctified by its association with death, although at no point is death even mentioned. In fact, it is an affirmation of life which proclaims the eternity of God, His grace and His sovereignty, and demands peace on Earth. When our faith is most tested (at the incomprehensible moment of death), we praise God and affirm our desire to unify a broken world. That is, in the face of adversity, we demand goodness and a better world. The words and, especially if one does not understand the text, the rhythm, bring together mourners with other mourners who have experienced a similar loss. The entire prayer is in Aramaic, with the exception of the final verse, which is in Hebrew.

Kahal "Congregation." It refers to the Jewish community in medieval Europe.

Karaites From the Hebrew word *"kara,"* which means the "reader of Scriptures," it refers to the group that opposed the rabbinic tradition in the 8th century C.E. and criticized the idea of Oral Law.

Kashrut The dietary laws.

Kavanah "Intention." It refers to the concentration that is required for a prayer to have meaning.

Kedushah A prayer that proclaims the holiness of God. It is recited on the Sabbath and holidays.

Kehilla "Community." The Jewish sense of community; a specific community within a global community.

Keriah The tearing of clothes upon hearing of the death of a close relative. Today, many Jews buy prefabricated torn cloth instead of tearing their own clothes.

Ketubah The wedding certificate or contract.

Ketuvim "Writings," section of the Bible.

Kibbutz A communal settlement in contemporary Israel.

Kiddush A prayer of holiness recited over wine to sanctify the Sabbath or another holiday.

Kippah Skull cap. The Yiddish word *"yarmulkah"* is also used.

Kittel A white shroud which the deceased are wrapped in, also worn by some during the *Yom Kippur* services to symbolize the new life that they are beginning after having cast away their sins.

Klaf The hand-written sheet placed inside the *Mezuzah*. It contains Deuteronomy 6:4-9 and 11:13-21.

K'lal Yisrael The Jewish People, the "community of Israel."

Knesset "Assembly." The contemporary Israeli Parliament.

Kodesh "Holy."

Kol Nidre "All the vows." On the eve of *Yom Kippur*, a prayer is recited in which we ask for the dispensation of vows which we had assumed as individuals for ourselves alone during the previous year and which we were unable to fulfill. The stirring tune of *Kol Nidre* is as famous as the prayer itself and the eve of *Yom Kippur* is referred to as *"Kol Nidre"* Night." It does not refer to vows made between us and other people.

Kosher/Kasher Adjective stating that a given food is allowed according to the dietary laws. The dietary laws are taken from the Bible and explained in detail in the Talmud.

Kugel A baked pudding with noodles or potatoes.

L

Ladino The colloquial language spoken by Sephardic Jews, based on Spanish with Hebrew and Arabic words and written using the Hebrew alphabet. Even today the descendants of Spanish Jews, who now live in the countries that took them in when they were expelled from Spain in 1492, speak this language.

Latke A fried food made of potatoes and eggs eaten during *Chanukah*.

Law of Return Israeli law which allows all Jews to immigrate to Israel and acquire Israeli citizenship.

L'chaim A toast meaning "To life."

Lecha Dodi Song composed in the 16th century by Solomon Alkabetz which welcomes the "Sabbath Bride."

Lehitpalel "To judge oneself." To pray.

L'Shanah Tova Tikatevu Greeting used between *Rosh HaShanah* and *Yom Kippur*. It literally means "May you be inscribed (in the Book of Life) for a good year." Frequently, one simply says "*Shanah Tova.*"

Lulav A palm branch decked with sprigs of willow and myrtle. They serve as symbols of the realm of vegetation along with the *etrog*, which is a citron. They are the characteristic feature of the morning service of *Sukkot*. The myrtle and willow sprigs are tied together with the palm branch and are held in the right hand, while the citron is held in the left hand when a special blessing is recited. They symbolize God's abundant blessings on Earth. The four species are waved during the recitation of *Hallel* (psalms of praise) in the direction of the four points of compass as well as upward and downward to symbolize the stream of abundance which comes from the heavens and the four directions of the Earth.

M

Ma'ariv The evening service. See also *"Arvit."*

Machzor Prayer book for the High Holy Days.

Magen David "The shield of David." This 6-point star became the symbol of Judaism after the 12th century.

Mame-loshn In Yiddish, "mother tongue." It refers to Yiddish.

Mamzer The child of a forbidden marriage. A bastard.

Maror The spicy horseradish used during *Pesach* which symbolizes the bitter life of the Israelite slaves in Egypt.

Marranos Pejorative term used in Spain during the Middle Ages to refer to Jews who forcibly converted to Christianity and secretly practiced Judaism. They were one of the targets of the Inquisition. Conversion was necessary to avoid being expelled after 1492.

Mashiach Centuries ago it referred to the descendent of King David who would redeem the world, bringing peace, justice, and abundance. The concept was developed in different ways over time. It was believed that the Messianic Age would be the time of the perfection of human institutions; others believed that it would be the time of radical changes, of a new order after the destruction of the world as we know it. But in Judaism the figure of the Messiah is not God.

Matzah The unleavened bread or the bread of affliction which reminds us of the hardships that the Hebrews endured in Egypt, and the fact that they did not have time to cook the bread in their haste to flee Egypt. Eaten during *Pesach*.

Mazal Tov Hebrew and Yiddish term meaning "Congratulations."

Megillah "Scroll," used to describe the 5 scrolls read during the holidays: *Sukkot*: *Kohelet* (Ecclesiasts); *Purim*: Esther; *Pesach*: *Shir HaShirim* (Song of Songs); *Shavuot*: Ruth; *Tishah B'Av*: *Eichah* (Lamentations).

Menorah The 7-arm candelabrum. It was used in the Temple of Jerusalem, and today it is a decorative object.

Mezuzah "Door post." This is perhaps the most important symbol of Judaism. It marks a Jewish home. It is an object that consists of a box with a *Klaf* inside. The box is affixed on an angle, with the top side facing the inside of the house, to the right of the door to the house, about two-thirds the way up (in some homes, there is a *mezuzah* on each door, except doors leading to bathrooms, among other restrictions). The *Klaf* contains the *Sh'ma* (Deuteronomy 6:4-9 and 11:13-21).

Mi Chamocha A hymn, "Who Is like You," which proclaims the wonders God performed for Israel. From these words comes the proper name "Michael."

Midrash It means "to inquire." A *midrash* is the explanation of the matter being examined and it refers to the commentary literature developed in classical Judaism which aims to interpret Scripture, to fill in the gaps. The word refers both to a specific *midrash* and to the body of midrashic literature.

Mikvah A ritual bath used for spiritual purification.

Milchig Yiddish for "milk." It describes the foods that contain dairy products and, therefore, cannot be mixed with meat.

Mincha The afternoon service.

Minyan A group of ten Jews (male Jews, according to the Orthodox) over 13 years old, necessary to say certain prayers.

Mishnah "Teaching." The body of Oral Law that existed at the end of the 2nd century and was collected, edited, and revised by Rabbi Judah HaNasi. It is the legal tradition of the wise men of two thousand years ago and represents the foundation of Talmudic discourse.

Mitzvah An obligation or commandment. There is a total of 613 *mitzvot* for Jews (and 7 for non-Jews: the "Noahide Laws"). Traditionally it was taught that by observing the *mitzvot* we would speed up the coming of the Messiah, and that observant Jews act as a "light unto the nations." The idea of the *mitzvot* is very important in Jewish history and helps to explain the phenomenon of the survival of the Jewish People throughout history. It also helps to explain the fact that Judaism is not a proselytizing religion. Why would somebody want to observe 613 commandments if he or she only needed to observe 7? Rabbi Simlaiu (3rd century C.E.) came up with the number 613. He divided them into 365 negative *mitzvot* (the number of days in a year) and 248 positive ones (which supposedly is the number of organs in a human body). This systematic nature has become a kind of Hebrew numerology, known as "*Gematria*," one of the 32 systems of text interpretation applied to the Torah in the Talmud and in *Midrash*, which assigns a numerical value to each letter.

Mohel A specialist who performs circumcisions.

Motzi Blessing of the bread, recited before eating.

Musaf The service that follows immediately after *Shacharit* on the Sabbath and holidays.

N

Neilah "Closing," referring to the symbolic closing of the gates of repentance at the conclusion of *Yom Kippur.* The final prayer service on *Yom Kippur* is called *"Neilah."*

Ner Tamid The "Eternal Light" that burns over the *Aron Kodesh.* It is a visual manifestation of the eternal light of the Torah, with all its implications (continual study, etc.).

Nevi'im "Prophets," section of the Bible.

O

Olam HaBa "The world to come." The life of the soul after death.

Omer The measure of grain offered in the Temple during Passover and the 16th day of *Nisan.* It is also, therefore, the name of the period of seven weeks between Passover and *Shavuot.*

Oneg Shabbat "The joy of the Sabbath." The informal gathering after Friday services which normally includes food and drink.

Oral Law According to the rabbinic tradition, God revealed instructions on how to live in the written Torah and a process of oral traditions.

P

Parasha The Torah portion read each week in the synagogue following an annual cycle. It is also known as the *Sidrah.*

Pareve In Yiddish, "neutral." It refers to foods that are neither diary nor meat products and, therefore, can be mixed with either. Fish, for instance, is *pareve.*

Parochet The curtain covering the *Aron Kodesh*.

Pesach Passover, the most important spring holiday. It commemorates the Exodus from Egypt. It lasts for eight days. During this holiday, Jews abstain from eating any fermented product. A ritual dinner is prepared (*Seder*) the first two nights during which the traditional narrative (*Hagdadah*) is retold.

Peshat An interpretative method used to read the Torah based on the literal meaning of the text.

Piku'ach Nefesh The principle according to which saving a life is more important than any ritual obligation and which supplants all prohibitions except idolatry, murder, and immoral behavior.

Pirke Avot A treatise of *Mishnah* that deals with ethical and moral conduct.

Pogrom An unprovoked attack or series of attacks against the Jewish community.

Purim A festival which commemorates the salvation of the Jews in Persia, described in the Book of Esther.

Purimspiel A comical play which "debuts" on *Purim*.

Pushke A box in the synagogue or at home used to collect money for charity.

R

Rabbi "My teacher." The rabbi is an expert on Jewish rituals and law, an authorized teacher, a figure that emerged after the destruction of the Second Temple (70 C.E.). His or her role has changed throughout history, and continues to change according to the needs of the Jewish community. Traditionally, he was the spiritual and legal leader of his community. The fundamental aspect of a rabbi's training is study. It is worth remembering that a rabbi is very different than a priest, a position that does not exist in Judaism. Rabbis are chosen by each congregation, which looks for a rabbi who personifies its values. Moreover, since sacraments do not exist in Judaism, a community does not need to have a rabbi for the vast majority of rituals. Nevertheless, the figure of the rabbi has been crucial in the perpetuation of the Jewish tradition.

Rebbe The title of the spiritual guide of the *Chassidim*.

Rebbetzin Yiddish for the rabbi's wife.

Responsa Answers to questions related to *Halacha*, written by the authorities. They are still written today to revise older ideas as the changes caused by the passage of time require new answers.

Rosh Chodesh "New month." The holiday of the new moon.

Rosh HaShanah "New Year." *Rosh HaShanah* is the new year in relation to creation but not the new year in relation to the calendar year, for *Rosh HaShanah* occurs in the month of *Tishri*, which is the 7th month of the calendar year. *Rosh HaShanah* is observed for 2 days in Israel as well as in America (except by the Reform movement, which observes only one day).

S

Sandak The person who holds the baby during his circumcision.

Sanhedrin From the Greek word meaning "assembly." It refers to the legislative and judicial body comprised of 71 members which existed until rabbinic times.

Seder "Order," referring to the order of the dinner which takes place on the first two nights of *Pesach* and is explained in the *Haggadah*.

Sefardim The descendants of the Jews of Spain, Portugal, and northern Africa before the expulsion from Spain in 1492. Culturally, it refers to the customs of this group. Although this term is used in contraposition to the *Ashkenazim,* one should not think that all Jews belong to one of these two groups. Italian and Ethiopian Jews, for instance, have created their own customs.

Sefer Torah A Torah scroll.

Selichot The prayers of repentance read on the midnight before *Rosh HaShanah.*

Shabbat The Sabbath. The seventh day of the week which commemorates the end of the creation of the world and the Exodus from Egypt. It symbolizes a new beginning and is dedicated to God. It is a sacred day of rest. The tone must be happy.

Shabbat Shalom The Sabbath greeting meaning "the peace of the Sabbath." In Yiddish, the greeting is *"Gut Shabbos."*

Shacharit The morning service.

Shalach Manot The custom of sending food or sweets to friends on *Purim.*

Shalom Bayit The principle according to which domestic peace must be guaranteed; the home is a sanctuary of peace and respect.

Shaloshim The 30-day period of mourning which includes the *Shivah* period.

Shamash The candle that lights the other *Chanukah* candles. It also refers to the person who cares for a cemetery.

Shavuot "Weeks." It is also known as the "Festival of First Fruits" because it is celebrated fifty days after the first offering of grain to the priests. It celebrates the moment God gave the Torah to Moses.

Shehecheianu "(God) has kept us alive." It is the blessing for beginnings and, in general, any joyous moment of one's life, such as the birth of a child and marriage. It is also said when lighting candles and when *Kaddish* is recited, among other moments.

Shemini Atzeret The "eight days of assembly." It is the 8th day of *Sukkot* but is a holiday in its own right. It is on this day that the prayer for rain is recited.

Sh'mone Esre "Eighteen." The central section of prayers recited while standing, with nineteen (not eighteen) "blessings": praises (1) of the God of the patriarchs, (2) of the power and (3) holiness of God; prayers for (4) knowledge, (5) repentance, (6) forgiveness, (7) redemption, (8) the curing of the sick, (9) agricultural prosperity, (10) the end of the Diaspora, (11) the judgement of the righteous, (12) the punishment of the wicked and heretics, (13) the reward for the pious, (14) the reconstruction of Jerusalem, (15) the restoration of the House of David, (16) the acceptance of prayers, (17) the graces of God, (18) the restoration of the Temple, and (19) peace.

Shemot The Book of Exodus.

Shivah The 7-day period of mourning after the death of a close relative. It begins on the day of burial. A series of rituals surrounds this period, rituals which address the pain of the mourner and his or her psychological needs.

Sh'ma The first word of what can be considered the central prayer in Judaism, which proclaims monotheism. It is found in Deuteronomy 6:4. God is one and unique. It is recited daily, in addition to Deuteronomy 6:5-9, 11:13-21, and Numbers 15:37-41, among other passages. It is written on the *Mezuzah*. In public services it is recited together, and the congregants usually cover their eyes when they begin reciting it, as a sign of the deep intention of the prayer.

Shoah The Hebrew word for the Holocaust.

Shofar The horn which is sounded on *Rosh HaShanah* (if it doesn't fall on *Shabbat*) and at the end of *Yom Kippur*. The *Shofar* is also sounded every morning the entire month preceding *Rosh HaShanah*. The *Shofar* is normally made of a ram's horn and the notes of the *Shofar* proclaim the sovereignty of God and symbolically call men to repentance. The sounds produced by the *Shofar* are the plain *Tekiah*, ending abruptly; the broken *Shevarim*, consisting of three short sounds; and the *Teruah*, a succession of tremulous sounds equal to three *Shevarim*.

Shomrim The people who remain with a corpse between death and burial, as a sign of respect to the dead, who should not be left alone.

Shtetl From Yiddish (pl. *shtetlach*). A small village in Eastern Europe where Jews lived. They ceased to exist after the second World War. These villages were very poor and were located in the Pale of Settlement, a wasteland, the only area the Jews were allowed to live.

Shul Yiddish for "synagogue."

Shulchan Aruch A compilation of laws related to Jewish rituals, edited by Joseph Caro in the 16th century. It is considered authoritative by Orthodox Jews.

Siddur "To order." The prayer book used in the synagogue for all services except certain holidays. See also *Machzor*.

Sidrah The Torah section read during a given week. Also known as the *Parasha*.

Simchat Torah "Rejoicing over the Torah." It immediately follows the holiday of *Shemini Atzeret* and is in many ways the most joyous celebration of the year. The reading of the Torah is completed and the cycle of the reading of the coming year is immediately begun again. The services are characterized by dancing and singing with the Torah and playful pranks and jokes are acceptable parts of the celebration. The Torahs are marched around the synagogue seven times and the children follow the processional with flags and apples, singing and dancing their way. The greeting is *"Yom Tov"* or *"Chag Sameach."* This holidays reminds us that everything is contained in the Torah, and that life means constant studying. It reflects the central importance of the Torah and of study in Judaism.

Sofer "Scribe." Traditionally, it was an academic, a researcher whose task it was to study and teach Jewish tradition. After the first century C.E., the *sofer* was no longer an academic, but rather a kind of civil servant and teacher of children. Today, it refers to the person who writes Torah scrolls.

Sukkah "Booth." A temporary structure with at least three walls and a roof covered with twigs and leaves. The walls must be sufficiently strong to withstand ordinary gusts of wind. The shade produced by the roof-covering (in Hebrew called *"S'chach"*) must exceed the amount of sunlight that penetrates but the stars must be visible through the roof-covering. The *Sukkah* is a historical reminder of the period of Jewish history when the Jews wandered through the desert for forty years before entering the promised land of Israel. During the wandering they lived in temporary booths. The frail *Sukkah* is said to convey symbolically the idea that man should never be haughty. It is a *Mitzvah* to "dwell" in the *Sukkah* during the holiday of *Sukkot*. To dwell is interpreted in different ways. Minimally it means to enter the *Sukkah* on the first night, to make *Kiddush* over the wine, to make the prayer over the bread, and to sit down in the *Sukkah* and eat. (There is also a special blessing recited upon sitting down in the *Sukkah*.) Maximally it means literally to live in the *Sukkah*. One eats all his or her meals and sleeps in the *Sukkah* the entire length of the holiday.

Sukkot The festival of the booths is seven days long. It falls on the 15th of the Hebrew month of *Tishri*, which is just days after *Yom Kippur*. It has both an historical and agricultural basis. Historically, it commemorates the Jews' wandering in the desert for forty years, and agriculturally it is the feast of the ingathering of the harvest.

Sufganiyot Fried dough filled with marmalade, served in Israel during *Chanukah.*

Synagogue The central institution of the Jewish community. A place of gathering: for services, study, etc.

T

Tallit Or *Tallis.* A rectangular prayer shawl with fringes (*Tzitzit*) and special knots at the ends. It is worn during morning services. The fringes, according to Numbers 15:38-39, remind the wearer of the commandments of God. According to tradition, males are buried with their *tallit,* but with the fringes cut from them.

Tallit Katan A square garment made of wool or silk to which fringes are added and which has a circular opening in the middle. It is put on over the shoulders and is worn by men under their "secular" clothes. Orthodox Jews always wear it.

Talmud "Study." Rabbinic Judaism produced two Talmuds: the Palestinian or Jerusalem Talmud (edited in the 4th century C.E.) and the Babylonian Talmud (edited in the 5th century C.E.). The latter has had a greater impact on Jewish life, primarily because it is more complete, since the editors had more time to finish their job. Both contain a collection of *Mishnah* by the *Tanaim,* as well as commentaries and debates (*Gemara*) by the *Amoraim.* The importance and impact that the Talmud has had cannot be overestimated. It is not a simple collection of laws and commentaries, but rather it reflects the Jewish way of being, including basic details such as the way to debate. Not only has it survived for centuries in all parts of the world, but also is the most important text with regard to Jewish identity in the Diaspora.

Tanaim "Repeaters." The wise men of the Hillel period until the compilation of the *Mishnah* (200 C.E.). They were the creators of the *Mishnah*.

Tanach The Jewish Bible, which consists of three parts: Torah (Pentateuch, or "five books"), *Nevi'im* (Prophets), and *Ketuvim* (Writings).

Tashlich "You will cast." It is the custom of symbolically casting the sins into a running body of water on the first day of *Rosh HaShanah* (on the second day if the first day falls on the *Shabbat*).

Tefilah "Prayer."

Tefilin Jewish law demands that all men older than 13 years old wear *Tefilin* during morning services (except on the Sabbath and holidays). They are made up of two square leather boxes that contain certain passages from the Bible. One is placed on the forehead, and the other on the left arm, near the heart. Long strips of leather are attached to each box. The box placed on the forehead has four compartments, each containing biblical passages. The box placed on the arm only has one compartment, which contains the four biblical passages. The passages deal with the oneness of God and the responsibility to love Him.

Teshuvah "Returning," but is often translated as "repentance." Repentance in Judaism entails a process of returning for it is not sufficient merely to admit one's sins but one must also take steps to correct the mistakes made and right the wrongs perpetrated. One cannot repent for a wrong against his fellow man by asking God for forgiveness. One must approach the person and ask for forgiveness and if possible compensate the person for the damage done. Repentance is never perfect and that is why we have *Rosh HaShanah* and *Yom Kippur* every year.

Tikkun Olam "To repair the world." The Jewish concept according to which Jews, as members of the human family, have the responsibility to contribute to the welfare of the broken and fragmented world.

Tisha B'Av The 9th of *Av*. A 24-hour fast which commemorates the destruction of both Temples as well as other catastrophes in Jewish history.

Torah "Teaching" or "instruction." In general, it refers to the study of the entire Jewish tradition, in the broadest sense. In a stricter sense, it refers to the five books of Moses in the Bible.

Treif It refers to non-*Kosher* foods.

Tzeddakah "Justice." It refers to acts of charity and philanthropy. It should not be confused with the Christian concept of charity, an act of love towards the poor, since the central idea for Judaism is responsibility, justice: not to make the situation more bearable, but to change it.

Tzitzit The fringes worn on a *Tallit*.

V

Vayikra The Book of Leviticus.

Y

Yad "Hand." A pointer in the shape of a hand used to read the Torah.

Yahrzeit The anniversary of the death of a close relative. In Yiddish, it means "a year." Many Jews light a candle on the eve of the anniversary. Psalms having something to do with the funeral service are recited; other prayers and meditations are found in *Siddurim* (pl. of *Siddur*). On the preceding Sabbath, the mourner is normally called up for an *Aliyah*. *Kaddish* is recited. Many people visit the cemetery around this time and give to charity.

Yamim Nora'im The "Days of Awe." This is the term that refers to the Holy Days of *Rosh HaShanah* and *Yom Kippur*. They are Days of Awe because on these days we are judged (or we judge ourselves) for our past deeds.

Yeshiva A rabbinical academy of advanced studies.

Yiddish The language of the *Ashkenazim*, a mix of several languages, especially German and Hebrew.

Yizkor A service in the synagogue that remembers the deceased on *Yom Kippur, Shemini Atzeret*, and the last days of *Pesach* and *Shavuot*. It normally takes place during the morning after the Torah service. The service was introduced during the Christian Crusades and the medieval pogroms in order to remember the massacred Jews. With time, it became a service to remember all Jews killed because they were Jews, as well as deceased relatives. The word *"Yizkor"* is the first word of the prayer. Other prayers, such as the *Kaddish*, are also recited. Many Jews take advantage of this opportunity to give to charity in the name of the deceased relative. A special candle is normally lighted on the eve of the service.

Yom HaAtzma'ut Israeli Day of Independence.

Yom HaShoah Day which remembers the horrors of the Holocaust.

Yom Kippur "Day of Atonement." A 25-hour fast period which is the culmination of the 10 Days of Repentance. It is the most solemn day of the Jewish calendar and the day is spent in prayer. The themes of the prayers are mainly the failings of man and the majesty of God. Forgiveness for sins against God is asked and we pray for a healthy and happy new year.

Yom Yerushalayim Celebrates the reunification of Jerusalem in 1967.

Z

Zionism In ancient Hebrew, "Zion" meant "Jerusalem." The name given to the non-religious concept of the reestablishment of Israel as a homeland for the Jews.

Zohar Literally, "The Book of Splendor." The main work of the Kabbalists.

Notes